HEALED *by* HORSES

HEALED
by
HORSES

A Memoir

❖

Carole Fletcher

with Lawrence Scanlan

ATRIA PRESS

New York   London   Toronto   Sydney

Photograph appearing on p. 1 of the insert (top, right) is courtesy of Saul Kushner; photograph appearing on p. 2 of the insert (top, right) is courtesy of Carl Emerick; photographs appearing on p. 5 of the insert (top) and p. 6 of the insert (bottom) are courtesy of Chris Sartre; photograph appearing on p. 7 of insert (top) is courtesy of Serita C. Hult; photograph appearing on p. 7 of insert (middle) is courtesy of *Ocala Magazine*/Payam Rahimian; photograph appearing on p. 7 of insert (bottom) is courtesy of Stan Phaneuf; all photographs appearing on p. 8 of the insert are courtesy of Michelle Younghans.

All other photographs are courtesy of Carole Fletcher

ATRIA BOOKS

1230 Avenue of the Americas
New York, NY 10020

Library of Congress Cataloging-in-Publication Data

Fletcher, Carole.
Healed by horses : a memoir / Carole Fletcher ; with Lawrence Scanlan.—
1st Atria Books hardcover ed.
p. cm
ISBN-10: 1-4165-8296-7
ISBN-13: 978-1-4165-8296-0

1. Fletcher, Carole. 2. Burns and scalds—Patients—United States—Biography.
3. Burns and scalds—Patients—Rehabilitation—United States.
I. Scanlan, Lawrence. II Title.
RD96.4.F56 2005
617.1'106'092—dc22
[B]   2004059555

First Atria Books hardcover edition April 2005

10 9 8 7 6 5 4 3 2 1

ATRIA BOOKS is a trademark of Simon & Schuster, Inc.

Manufactured in the United States of America

For information regarding special discounts for bulk purchases, please contact Simon & Schuster Special Sales at 1-800-456-6798 or business@simonandschuster.com

For my mother, Jene.

And to the memory of my horse, Dial.

HEALED *by* HORSES

Introduction

FOLLOWING THE EVENTS of September 11 in 2001, President George W. Bush and First Lady Laura Bush toured the burn unit at Washington Hospital Center.

Dr. Robert Lowery, who accompanied the president, would later describe how "one of the burn patients, breathing through a tube connected to a ventilator, was swathed in gauze, like a mummy, with only eyes, lips, fingers, and toes visible. The odor of burns, dressings, and body fluids was strong. Even before the president went into the first patient's room, he was visibly shaken. . . . When he turned my way, I saw a man different from the man who greeted us."

Dr. Lowery's words were set down in the winter 2001 issue of *Burn Support News,* a national newsletter published by the Phoenix Society for Burn Survivors. The phoenix was the mythical bird that would live for centuries, allow itself to be consumed by fire, and then rise, restored and renewed, from the ashes.

Carole Fletcher knows all about rising from ashes and the smell of burn units; a stained-glass window depicting a phoenix is among her most prized possessions. On November 22, 1975, she was helping friends rebuild an engine in the basement of her house in New Jersey when the pilot light on a water heater ignited gasoline fumes. On that day, at the age of twenty-eight, she joined a large, mostly silent group. Each year, some 2.4 million burn injuries are reported in America, with 42 percent of cases resulting in substantial or permanent disabilities. This grim accounting includes more than 20,000 men, women, and children who suffer life-threatening burns—from car crashes, industrial explosions, mishaps with fireplaces and grills, encounters with stoves and boiling water.

Carole Fletcher can talk—almost with equanimity—about the long and torturous road from disabled and disfigured burn victim to what she is now: an internationally prominent trick-horse trainer and performer. At her farm in Florida, she and I went through a drawer full of photographs. Some families arrange pictures in neat albums, the images dated and captioned and tucked behind plastic sleeves. The horse people I know—spotless though their barns and tack rooms may be—have no time for organizing photo albums. (Tack rooms house saddles, bridles, blankets, and other riding gear.) Carole Fletcher's entire life, before and after the accident, lay willy-nilly in that deep wide drawer.

Two images stayed with me long afterward. One, a professionally shot eight-and-a-half-by-eleven portrait in black and white, shows a striking young woman in a 1960s beehive, elegantly dressed as if for an evening out. She seems a tad serious, but the eyes are bright and luminous, the lashes long, the lips sculpted, the skin flawless. She is eighteen and looks a little like Audrey Hepburn; no, prettier. *My Fair Lady* indeed. Carole Fletcher was a classically trained pianist, a charm school graduate, a prom queen.

Another image, this one a family snapshot with a curious sepia tone, like a blend of blood and brandy, shows Carole in the burn unit. Hackensack Medical Center in New Jersey was a place she would call home for seven consecutive months; other surgeries, at Massachusetts General in Boston, would eventually bump her total time in the hospital to three years. In the photograph, Carole has pulled the sheets over her ravaged mouth, so the focus is all on the eyes. Eyes that so sparkled in the other photograph now convey loss and anger, hurt from what she has already endured and worry over what else the surgeons have in store. There is fatigue in those eyes, and they are vaguely accusatory ("Why me?" they ask), but I see gritty determination there too. As for the pain—and I mean here the pure physical pain and not all the other kinds, emotional, psychological, spiritual, that then assailed her unrelievedly—it is beyond my imagining. It struck me how matter-of-fact she some-times was in her recounting of events, like a veteran shielding a young listener from the truth of war. You had to coax a little, and then it came.

Seeking to fathom her experience, I tried for a foothold. I told Carole that as a fair-skinned child, a red-haired, freckled boy of Irish descent, I suffered severe sunburns on my arms and neck and shoul-ders, burns that would erupt into tapioca-sized blisters. My skin was so fair I would burn through the cotton of a shirt. At night, I would set up bookbinders—the zippered cases pupils then used to haul notes and textbooks—on either side of my bed. The makeshift rig was meant to protect me against the chill without the sheet touching my skin.

"Because of the pain of touch," said Carole.

"Yes," I replied. "Because of the pain," one I can conjure now, more than four decades later.

"Now imagine having *no* skin," she said. "Imagine the pain of any kind of touch." Imagine, she was saying, the small hurt of a sunburn, then magnify it. Make it grow into a mountain.

It was all those burn-unit smells—the primary one of rank, infected flesh and the indescribable tang of newly grafted skin, the head-back bracing smell of iodine and Betadine and other antiseptic solutions, the pungent smell of alcohol foretelling needles, the familiar, tiresome whiff from catheters and bedpans—that made Carole yearn for other smells. The ones she associated with the barn where her horse was stabled. The aroma of sweet-smelling hay gathered in a barn or, even better, fresh-cut grass in a pasture. The musky smell of leather, especially oiled leather, in a tack room. The smell of molasses, in sweet feed or drizzled on bran mash. The perfume of pine shavings. The liberating smells of dust and dirt and horse manure. The smell of a wet horse, as pure as rain. And that earthy scent you get when you press your head into a horse's mane. At the time of the accident, horses were merely a hobby for Carole Fletcher, like tennis or sailing. That would change. If the burn unit smelled of loss and despair, the barn would come to offer the fresh and unmistakable scent of hope.

During all those months that Carole Fletcher spent in the burn unit, "in airless hospital rooms invariably painted yellow or green," she kept conjuring the barn, where the sound of birds filtered in, the wind riffled through the trees, and crickets called to one another in the surrounding fields. The barn would become not just a source of sensory pleasure but a refuge, a world apart.

We were to meet at baggage pickup in the Orlando airport, and though I had seen pictures of Carole, I managed not to recognize her. It was only when I saw the scar tissue on the backs of her legs that I was emboldened to ask, "Carole Fletcher?"

The pictures I had seen showed her on her trick horse, Night Train, him pawing the air like Trigger and Carole dolled up like Dale Evans. Carole has written a book and produced a video series on trick-horse training, given clinics all over the country, and performed in thousands of shows. In my mind's eye, she was raven-haired and tall in every way. "Dale Evans on a mission," as she once described herself.

But the woman at the airport was tiny as a bird, five feet, two inches tall with the skinny bird legs of a killdeer. She is fifty-five, but her whole bearing is that of a much younger woman. Her strawberry blond hair is gathered in a ponytail, and she has a kind of whirligig walk—her short legs shuffle, her elbows are cocked and busy, her gaze is straight ahead in the style of the marathon walker. The eyes are blue, bright, and alert. The *My Fair Lady* sparkle is there yet.

Transportation is a 1995 Ford F350 Turbo Diesel with 128,000 miles on it, most of them from hauling horses all over the country. The Fletchers have a car, but it's an aged Oldsmobile, and they don't trust it very much. Carole capably handles the big white truck (horsemen call these double-axle trucks duallies), though in it she looks like a child on a draft horse's back.

Carole would drive me back to the same airport a week later, by which time two truths had become abundantly clear. One, here was an extraordinary woman with uncommon optimism and energy and appetite for life. To call her a morning person fails to capture her *carpe diem* up-and-at-'em philosophy: she rises at 5:00 A.M., saying "I can't *wait* to get up in the morning, to get out there at first light and feed my horses, to chat with them in that quiet time and begin working with them." As for the "bird" legs, Carole's husband Gary sets me straight. "She has short legs and thunder thighs," he jokes. All that work around horses, riding, hauling hay, has made her deceptively strong.

Second, it is no vague or romantic notion to suggest that horses—Bailey first, then Dial, then the several hundred horses who came after them, horses named Angel Eyes and Cheyenne Spring and Night Train and all the rest—saved her life. Giving riding lessons, training young horses for riding and "trickonometry" (trick-horse training), performing with her horses at shows and clinics, building up vast reservoirs of patience and perseverance—all this revived her. A life built around horses quite literally brought Carole Fletcher back from the brink.

❀   ❀   ❀

Marion County calls itself "the horse capital of the world," with more horses and ponies than any other county in the nation—and perhaps any other region on earth. Of Florida's seven hundred Thoroughbred farms and training centers, three-quarters are set in the rolling country around Ocala, where thirty-five thousand Thoroughbreds are registered. The wealth, the economic impact on Ocala, of purebred horses is measured in the billions.

Horse people here sometimes lament the fire ants, water moccasins, and alligators, the lightning strikes, and summer heat ("You think it's hot here" reads a religious billboard I saw from the highway, a warning to sinners, apparently signed by God), but the advantages are substantial. Year-round grazing means that horse owners with land never haul hay. Wells are deep; water is pure and plentiful. (It was in Florida that a Spanish conquistador, Juan Ponce de León quested for the fountain of youth.) Limestone in the ground lends nutrients to the grass and helps grow good bone in horses. The list of champion horses bred here is long: Silver Charm, winner of the Kentucky Derby and the Preakness in 1997; Skip Away, the thoroughbred North American Horse of the Year in 1998; Rugged Lark, twice named Super Horse by the American Quarter Horse Association. Finally, Marion County's majestic live oaks, with their spreading limbs and Spanish moss hanging in the breeze, lend a southern charm to every paddock that claims one. There is no more beautiful tree in all creation.

Carole Fletcher and her husband Gary came to Reddick, Marion County, in 1997. They left behind a stunning equestrian retreat they had built themselves in the woods of New Hampshire. One winter's day the weight of snow and ice collapsed their huge indoor riding ring, miraculously sparing the horses in adjoining stalls. Though they are not quitters—far from it—the Fletchers took the calamity as a sign. Carole had been coming to Marion County for years on horse-buying missions, and winterless weather finally proved irresistible.

The sign proclaiming "Singin' Saddles Ranch" in Florida is the same one that fronted their place in New Hampshire. The white pine slab (Gary cut the immense tree himself on their property) is more than twenty feet wide, several inches thick, and three feet from top to bottom. Blue rope letters routed out of the wood proclaim the ranch's name to visitors, who will then notice as they leave "Adios, y'all" etched into the sign's other side. To the right of the word *Ranch* is a guitar resting on a silver show saddle. Left of the word *Singin'* is a spotted brown-and-white paint horse head framed by a silver horseshoe—the points facing upward, of course, lest the luck all run out.

The name Singin' Saddles fits on several counts. When she was a girl, Carole was obsessed with cowboys—Gene Autry, the Singing Cowboy, for one. Carole would one day learn to play the guitar herself and perform in a bluegrass band. Even the blue of the rope seems right: Carole and Gary Fletcher, two of their dogs, and two of their horses are all blue-eyed. Finally, there is a cheeriness about the name Singin' Saddles that seems to suit the character of Carole Fletcher, though cheery defiance is perhaps closer to the mark.

As Florida farms go, the Fletcher outfit is modest, at ten acres. Other places around here—their gates resplendent with ornate fountains and bronze equestrian statues—spread over several thousand acres. Among Carole and Gary's neighbors are Pat Parelli, a luminary in the world of natural horsemanship (or "horse whisperers," as some call them) and Bruce Davidson, a world-class eventer with an Olympic gold medal on his shelf. The ditches around Reddick are twenty-foot-wide grassy lanes on either side of the road, and they are well stamped by horses' hooves and droppings.

In that aforementioned drawer were many photographs of Carole on horseback. One, taken several years after the fire, has Carole on Dial, her hat raised in the air, striking a note of muted triumph. The half-smile looks forced, the eyes defiant. Years later, another photograph. Carole on Night Train in front of her barn in New Hampshire. The assurance is back now, grimmer perhaps, but back. She looks so at home in the saddle, Night Train's blue eyes like beacons of light. Finally, a recent photo at the new place in Florida: Carole on the ground with a bowing palomino, her smile as wide as the ocean. The photo says, This is my realm, what I do, and I do it well.

Well back from the road, the Fletcher home is a sprawling ranch house, wide and long, rustic in a way, with Spanish and Mediterranean touches—rounded archways and cool tile floors, wooden beams. Its essential privacy must have appealed to its new owners, whose previous house commanded an imposing view of a solitary wooded valley in New Hampshire. The driveway leading to the house at Reddick passes paddocks on the right and dense forest on the left. Night Train, Carole's aging but still proud paint stallion, was grazing as I passed that first time. Then came a pond, home to a dozen or so geese and ducks, and full, I would later learn, of catfish. Several peacocks roam the place as peacocks do—like they own it. I would meet the three dogs, Australian shepherds named Dewey and Fancy and Roo; cats named Big Kitty, Katie, and Prince. And the horses, of course, the paints Night Train, Amigo, Angel Eyes, and Playboy.

There are many more horses in the house. There are horses on the kitchen tea towels, horses on the get-along-little-dogie wallpaper in the bathroom; the letter holder is horse-shaped, as is the cookie jar. There are Remington prints on the hallway walls and, in the foyer, a cowboy hat collection. Among Carole's most precious possessions is a Ted Flowers silver parade saddle, fifty years old and the kind used by the silver-screen cowboys.

In one corner of the guest bedroom where I slept is a life-size cutout of Dale Evans, a gift from someone whose horse Carole trained. Dale would have admired the rectangle of dark brown cowhide cut neatly into the headboard of the bed and the bold tapestry on the wall above: horses grazing in some ethereal pasture. In the dining room is a coterie of photos depicting Roy Rogers and Trigger (six in all) in one large frame, including one in which horse and rider are seated around a set table and poised to chow down a meal of carrots. The most remarkable shot shows Roy standing over Trigger's upturned form, the cowboy's right foot resting on the horse's left front hoof. (It's a maneuver only rarely accomplished and one that Carole has perfected with Playboy, her young trick horse in training.)

Sometimes she will talk to her horses in the gushy, simple, cooing language that some of us reserve for much-loved dogs. "What a good boyyyyyyyyyy," she will say to one—at the paddock fence, or in the course of a schooling session—and then punctuate it with a little *hah*. "Hold it, hold it, hold it. Yes. You are a prince. *Hah*. Yes, you are. *Hah*."

Playboy may be her prince, but he is also her pal. No, more than a pal. He and the other horses in her life, past and present, are the children Carole never had. She trains them much as she would rear a child—with respect and kindness and "an iron fist in a kid glove," to quote Glen Randall, a horse trainer she admires.

Horses changed Carole Fletcher's life. They gave her hope when there was very little to cling to. The story of her life is about the healing power of horses (the notion of animal therapy is one I'll come back to in the epilogue); it's also a tale about friendship. Carole has many friends, human and horse, and is sustained by both. The Good Book likewise praises friendship, though the author cannot have had the horse in mind, in the book of Ecclesiastes 6:16: "A faithful friend is the medicine of life."

—*Lawrence Scanlan*

1

The Early Years

A FAMILY PHOTO shows me, Carole Ann Rosenberg, at age seven in favored costume: cowboy hat, western dress, steer horn round my neck. I look doe-eyed and awestruck, for beside me are my heroes of the day, Gene Autry and his famous horse Champion— replete with tiny guns on his bit shanks and tack embossed with shining silver.

A neighbor on our street in suburban Teaneck, New Jersey— Claire Primus—was a journalist who had managed to get me backstage at Madison Square Garden to meet the legendary Singing Cowboy. I have a vivid memory of Gene strumming his guitar on his horse in the rodeo ring, Champion losing his balance, and his rider falling off the back end. Gene calmly dusted himself off and got back on while joking to the crowd that there must be an easier way to dismount than this. Afterward I met the Range Rider (Jock Mahoney), his sidekick Dick Jones, and the rodeo clowns who hid from the bulls in barrels, and got everyone's autograph.

In the evenings, I'd watch *Gunsmoke, Bonanza, Have Gun, Will Travel, Bat Masterson,* and *Rawhide.* I'd escape into the books whose horses had captured my heart—*My Friend Flicka, Black Beauty, National Velvet, The Black Stallion.* For years, I rode the bench in front of the piano. I even kept sugar cubes in my pocket on the off chance that I'd encounter a horse I could befriend.

As a child, I carried my Gene Autry thermos to school every day, along with my Roy Rogers lunchbox. I still have both thermos and lunchbox. They sit on a shelf in the living room, and visitors to our house invariably pick one up and hold it. For most people, the sight of Gene singing to Champion or of Roy with his hand on Trigger's face brings back memories.

I cannot remember when I did not love horses. Some of my earliest memories are of riding rocking horses for hours on end, and stick horses with yarn manes attached. I rode every carousel horse at fairs for as long as my parents would let me, and every mechanical horse in front of every store.

Starting at age six, I spent entire summers at camps in New York and Pennsylvania, in the Catskill and Pocono mountains, camps such as Camp Lakota, Camp Roosevelt, and Camp-with-a-Wind. I took to camp like a duck to water. I loved the daily horseback riding, waterskiing, and softball, and the camp musicals, in which I often played the lead (Sister Sarah in *Guys and Dolls,* Ado Annie in *Oklahoma,* Nellie in *South Pacific*). Here I was no longer a slave to the piano and the metronome. Here I was in the company of birds, fish, dogs, barn cats, horses. Close to nature, close to God.

At Rosenberg family reunions, I befriended my cousin Justine, three years my junior. She had a large pony named Ginger and a less-than-purebred Thoroughbred called Spring Fever. They were kept at the Fox Chase stables, where Caroline Kennedy kept her horse. I would pet or groom Spring Fever for as long as the horse would allow. Justine had the life I longed for but only dreamed of: her own horse, her mother's blessing. When I was a teenager and warring with my mother, I pleaded with her to let me go live with Uncle Eddie and Aunt Sarah in Short Hills, New Jersey. Surely they'd let me have a horse. My horse.

A suburban kid with a country heart, I had to console myself by living on the range vicariously with my favorite cowboys—Gene and Roy, the Lone Ranger, the Cisco Kid. I could recite the introductions to all their shows, knew their horses and their many tricks. There was Roy and his palomino Trigger, Dale Evans and her buckskin Buttermilk (along with their dog Bullet and jeep Nelliebelle). There was Gene and Champion, the Lone Ranger and his gray Silver ("A fiery horse with the speed of light, a cloud of dust and a hearty 'Hi-ho Silver.' Return with us now to those thrilling days of yesteryear. The Lone Ranger rides again!"), Tonto and his paint Scout (Kemosabe, Tonto's name for his ranger pal, was supposed to mean "trusted scout"). The Cisco Kid rode Diablo; Hoppy rode Topper; Annie Oakley rode Target.

I had a Roy Rogers guitar, a cutout doll book of Roy and Dale, and I knew the year Trigger was born: 1932. (Actually, there were at least five "Triggers" used during tours, movies, the television show, and promotional shots. Each was trained by Glen Randall, a man I would one day come to know, and each had his own special tricks. Gene Autry, similarly, used seven animals known as Champion during his career.)

Roy Rogers, Gene Autry, and the others may have been the stars of those old movies, but it was the cowboys' (and cowgirls') sidekick, the horse, that pulled the movie along. The horse would rescue the hero, whinny when trouble was near, untie ropes from wrists, chase the bad guys into a corner, kick guns from villains' hands or create a diversion when that was called for. The famous horses had their own fan clubs (I was a member of several) and, in some cases, their own comic books. Small wonder that when Roy Rogers signed photos, comics, books, and programs, it was always "Roy Rogers and Trigger."

The westerns showed me the ways of the West, but they also set down what I took to be moral codes, even commandments. The shows were morality plays that pitted good against evil, good guys in white hats against bad guys in black. I still have my Roy Rogers Rider Club card and thus can list the Roy Rogers Riders' Rules:

1. Be neat and clean.
2. Be courteous and polite.
3. Always obey your parents.
4. Protect the weak and help them.
5. Be brave but never take chances.
6. Study hard and learn all you can.
7. Be kind to animals and take care of them.
8. Eat all your food and never waste any.
9. Love God, and go to Sunday school regularly.
10. Always respect our flag and our country.

The first commandment posed no hurdle, but that was in part because we had a nanny, Mrs. Simons, who picked up after me and ensured I was neat and clean. She was a hefty woman with ample arms, warm and nurturing. In her fifties, with one grown son, she always wore aprons, bathed and fed me, watched me play, and took me for walks. She also made the best apple pies, and her chocolate cookies weren't too shabby either. I grew to love this gentle woman, my surrogate mother.

My own mother, Jene, was, and remains, a formidable woman. She was a working woman long before that phrase became fashionable, but as I grew up I increasingly resented her allegiance to her work—a string of women's wear stores. We were destined to clash, she and I, and we did. Roy Rogers's rule number three—Always obey your parents—would fall prey to our little war. My father, Irving, tried to keep the peace but was powerless. Bless him, he also made me laugh and let me into that other world, the one I longed for—the world of animals.

It was Roy Rogers rule number seven—Be kind to animals and take care of them—that I sought most to obey and the one that proved hardest to honor. Until I was eight years old and my brother Michael came along, I was an only, lonely child in the iron grip of my mother's perfumed hand.

Michael Steven was adopted as a newborn, and my welcoming remark was what you might expect from a child facing the prospect of sharing the limelight: "Why couldn't I have a puppy instead of a baby brother?" Later I would play with him and dress him up—as a cowboy, naturally. But the age gap, along with his physical and mental handicaps, place an insurmountable distance between us.

Michael, we would eventually learn, had a mild form of cerebral palsy that affected his motor skills and hand-eye coordination. As a toddler, he would walk on his toes, unable to place his feet flat on the ground. Doctors at the Mayo Clinic advised that he wear braces to stretch the tendons and muscles. Eventually he did walk properly, and his lazy eye was corrected by glasses. But he would never run and catch a ball like other children. And while my father did all he could to "make a man" of him (even employing a neighborhood boy to teach Michael how to ride a bike and fight those who teased him in the schoolyard), my mother coddled and pampered him. She hired tutors to help him with homework or did it herself. Often, Michael would retreat and bury himself in a comic book. Later it was fantasy and science fiction, Tolkien, *Star Trek,* and television.

Looking back, I imagine it must have been hard for my brother as a boy to compete with a sister who was an honor roll student, and voted most popular, best-looking, and best-dressed in eighth grade.

My parents' business—my father worked in the stores as well—eventually did well, prospering so much that we moved "uptown." Moved, that is, from a mill-town house on a lot so small you could hear your neighbor sneeze to the classy suburbs.

Our custom-made flagstone split-level ranch house was built on a hundred-foot-square lot that boasted a backyard with a small hill I could sled on in winter. The finished basement had a built-in bar and barbecue pit. There were automatic garage door openers, built-in lazy Susan cabinets throughout the kitchen, and a laundry chute that dropped laundry (and my toys) into the basement laundry room. My mother hired an interior decorator who deployed expensive antiques (vintage French) throughout the house.

Private schools, Broadway shows, and weekends in Catskill Mountains hotels were standard fare for our family. There was money, too, for lessons—ballet and tap dancing to the age of six, and piano, of course.

But not just any piano. It was a 1923 Steinway "M" baby grand, and my mother would tell all who cared to listen that it had been tuned by the same man used by Leonard Bernstein. From the age of six to the age of fifteen (when I finally rebelled), I practiced daily at that piano. My mother would time me.

"Tie you?" asked a friend to whom I recently told my tale. He was horrified, but he had misheard. Yet in a way, he heard right. My mother was an opera buff, and she had a notion that her daughter would become a concert pianist. She also dreamed in her youth of becoming a teacher, but that never happened. Instead, she foisted both dreams on me, and I wavered between doing all I could to please my mother and running in the other direction. For all intents and purposes, I was indeed tied to that piano by my mother's sturdy rope. Not to play would have been ungrateful. My mother had bought me a Steinway, after all, had layered on all that guilt and expectation, and it would have been churlish of me not to play.

My teacher was Grace Harrington, an instructor at the famed Juilliard School of Music and a pianist who had played at Carnegie Hall. I remember her shiny cheeks, the bun in her hair. Her metronome still rings in my ears. I was made to practice an hour daily, and then two hours daily—flowing up and down scales, studying theory, and sight-reading.

When I grew frustrated with this strict regime, as I often did, I would escape to the basement. It was there that my few animals were confined. My mother detested animals, likely because of some long-forgotten incident in her childhood.

As a child, I was not allowed a dog or a cat—despite all my pleas. Pets, my mother informed me, were dirty. They would have soiled her wall-to-wall beige carpeting or, worse, got up on the baby blue upholstered sectional. My animal friends, upstairs anyway, were a huge stuffed frog called Grasshopper and a stuffed chestnut pony who went by the name of Tony Pony. Neither posed a threat to the furniture.

My basement coterie included a turtle called Tomatohead, assorted fish, parakeets, and a parrot named Trixie, whom I taught to climb a toy ladder and follow a mirror. These animals were my best friends, and I'd talk to them and care for them daily. I was intrigued by God's wondrous creations and wanted to touch them and learn their every movement. I am both sad and grateful about this, but it's true: my animal friends were the most cherished of my childhood. Though I had friends and was well liked at school, I was lonely at home.

My father once smuggled into the basement a stray kitten I called Pretzel, after my father's favorite snack. The ruse was soon exposed by a live-in German maid named Ingrid who responded to the creature in her laundry basket with a string of words whose meaning I had no trouble guessing. Pretzel went to neighbors.

Tomatohead and the birds would have to do. Every day when I came home from school, I'd rush down to the basement, clean their cages, put in fresh seeds and nuts, fruit, and vegetables for the birds, and lettuce for the turtle. I'd let Tomatohead out of his cage and watch him crawl around the room from my perch on the sofa. I'd also let the birds out of their cages, taking pleasure in seeing them explore every nook and cranny of the basement. To my mother's horror, they also explored her coiffed, hair-sprayed, beauty parlor hairdo. I would caress their feathers and teach them how to talk—"Pretty boy" and "Hello" and, to my father's amusement, "Oh, crap!" (timed to coincide with my mother coming down the stairs to my animal kingdom).

I was just starting to experience the rich communication possible between human and animal.

2

On the Home Front

IF MY FIRST MEMORY is of being picked up as an infant by Lil Simons, the nanny we had the first few years of my life, my second is of being picked up and held by my father. Irving Rosenberg had blue eyes, Maxfield Parrish blue, with a twinkle, the kindest eyes in the world.

My father taught me to ride a bike, steer a boat, catch a fish, and ride a horse. He took me everywhere with him—to buy lumber, to get ice cream, skiing, skating, fishing, golfing. I called him, with affection, Big Foot—for his wide (triple-E) and troubled feet, a legacy of the war. In the frigid waters off Newfoundland, his ship had been torpedoed. He and eleven survivors clung to a raft, and he would spend almost a year recovering in a naval hospital. Phlebitis—a blood circulation problem—would plague him, and his wide feet, all his life.

I remember him in long-sleeved shirts—button-down khakis with the sleeves rolled up—and green pants. He loved his Buicks, his ginger ale and Canadian Club, his cigars and cigarettes (Camel at first, then Kent), and beer and steak and lobster; in his later years he grew thick at the waist. The cigarettes stained his fingers yellow and lent a little rasp to his voice, but its timbre remained soft.

He was about five feet, eight inches tall, of medium build. Though his smile was as wide as the stern of his boat, his back was a constant source of pain: boards under his mattress, sleeping on the floor, and Epsom salts baths were his various therapies. The smell of Bengay medicated ointment brings him back to me in a heartbeat; he would always leave the tube around, and one time I came home late and brushed my teeth with it. He used Vitalis in his wavy brown hair, worn flat against his head and parted on the left near the middle. I would tousle his hair and tease him about using the tonic long after it was fashionable.

He enjoyed telling jokes or leaving funny notes: on the fridge, on my pillow, in my lunchbox, in my drawer. He was a clown and a tease, and that twinkle in his eye meant he was either up to something or about to tell a joke. Fun (or was it pun?) was my father's middle name. "Seven days without laughing," he would say, "makes one weak." He would pass on to me his delight in puns, the worse the better. Pop was so easygoing, it was hard to make him angry; when he did get angry, you knew he was hurt. It was as easy for him to cry as it was for him to laugh.

Given his past, it was surprising that he was so nimble and cheery. He was the sixth of nine children in the home of Charles and Anna Truegerman Rosenberg. (Jewish tradition has it that a child be named after the deceased, and my name borrows from both Charles and Anna; thus, Carole Ann.) My grandparents had emigrated from a part of Russia then known as Bessarabia to escape the persecution of the Jews. Charles, a furrier, died in 1917 of a cerebral hemorrhage when my father was eight; Anna died of pneumonia when he was thirteen. My father and his four young brothers were suddenly orphans.

The oldest daughter, Sara, though she had three children of her own, took them in; her husband Phil—a boat painter and fisherman—became a surrogate and loving father. But the family of ten would have to be fed, and my father was put to work. He sold knishes (pastries filled with potatoes), hot dogs, and ice cream on the boardwalk at Coney Island. He had a newspaper route, worked as pin boy at a local bowling alley, and caddied at the golf course. He also worked with Phil on Phil's boat, and I would inherit both my father's work ethic and his passion for the ocean.

After his stint in the navy, my father met my mother, Jennie Weiss, at a dance, and after a year-long romance, they married. On February 24, 1947, when Jennie was thirty-one, she gave birth to a six-pound, six-ounce baby girl.

My mother tried to feminize me by including me in her modeling shows and making me wear pinafores, lacy dresses, and Mary Janes. But there was something of the tomboy in me; I preferred jeans, sneakers, and sweaters to learning what fork to use at the table. Dad and I would appear at dinner in shirts that reeked of fish and bait, or of ponies, my riding boots still proudly clumped with manure. This irked my mother (which was a bonus; irking my mother was always a bonus) and brought me closer to my father.

He had been a diver in the navy, a hunter who loved animals, an outdoorsman and sportsman who taught me how to throw a ball, roller-skate, play tennis, swim—and ride. He would hoist me onto ponies at local stables, in New Milford and Passaic County. Above all, he made time for me.

In summer, he'd take me to batting cages and driving ranges, and to Yankee Stadium in the Bronx to watch the Say Hey Kid, Willie Mays. He would take me to department stores for lunches and ice cream sodas. He would tip generously, for that was his way; my way, too. What he had, he shared. His motto was, "Go big, or stay home."

During the winter, my father would take me to the Rockefeller Center in New York City, and we'd skate in front of the huge Christmas tree. We'd eat hot roasted chestnuts from one of the street vendors, then wash them down with hot chocolate. Afterward we'd go to Radio City Music Hall and watch the magnificent Rockettes, all those shapely legs rising and dropping in precision. I would take home as a souvenir one of those plastic dome-shaped villages you shook to make it snow. How, I wondered, could a snowstorm be so magically confined under glass?

While still a young man, my father captained a boat that took fishing parties out on the ocean. Later, he would sell the *Lucky Lady* (as it was called) to help launch the lingerie business. Started in Paterson, New Jersey, the Corset Bar specialized in women's lingerie, swimsuits, and sportswear, and soon there was a string of such stores. A decade and much hard work later, my parents owned that sprawling ranch house on Sunderland Road in Teaneck, New Jersey, and a boat called *Miss Jene I* and, later, its successor, *Miss Jene*

II. These were wooden boats, cabin cruisers called Egg Harbors after their maker in Egg Harbor, New Jersey. The first incarnation slept four; the second model, six. Each had a flying bridge, a bar, and a shower, with custom woodwork on the deck.

During the war, my father brought my mother home to meet his family for the first time. My mother then managed Blackton's of Fifth Avenue, an upscale lingerie store (gone now). In her high heels, fancy hair, and polished nails, she was, they were sure, a floozy. Until she showed them how fast she could fillet a fish.

When she was a girl, my mother worked in her father's fish store in Paterson, New Jersey, the old silk mill town where I was born and lived the first five years of my life. My mother was born in 1916, the youngest daughter of five children in the cramped home of Solomon and Lilly Weiss. After Lilly won the Polish lottery, the two imigrated to America and started the fish business. The Depression hit, and the children had to work. Filleting smelly fish gave my mother a certain skill—and her prospective in-laws would be suitably impressed—but the experience caused her to set her career sights elsewhere. Fashion, perhaps? By the age of eighteen (though she claimed she was twenty-four when she was hired), she had a job at Blackton's.

I don't much recall the Weiss fish store, though I vividly recall Solomon Weiss. Solomon the Great, as some called him, was a small man with a menacing-looking goatee. He would speak Yiddish or Polish to my mother, who would translate. I recall him stamping his cane, but I do not recall him ever smiling. Where Lilly was frail and warm, a fine cook who always had a trinket for her grandchildren, my grandfather was stern. "His word," my mother would say, "was law." He was a general who begat a general—my mother.

Solomon's great hope was that his children would become wealthy and donate some of their riches to the synagogue, thereby raising his stature. He used to call me "princess" and my brother "Michael Millionaire," and he would brag about his children, as my mother would later brag about me.

But the religion that gave my grandfather and mother such comfort gave me none. I resented going to synagogue and dozed through the rabbi's sermons. He noticed, and one Friday evening pointed me out. "The girl I'm putting to sleep," the rabbi told the congregation, "will now lead us in song." As I grew older, I became convinced that my mother's faith was one of convenience. How, I asked myself, can a religious Jew work on Saturday—the Sabbath? How could she keep kosher traditions in her house (separate sets of dishes for dairy and meat) yet allow pork spare ribs and lobster (both forbidden in Jewish canon law) to be eaten in our house on paper plates?

Religion defined my mother's side of the family, but not my father's. It was as if I belonged to two tribes. Rosenberg family gatherings were always about fun (baseball in the park, sand castles on Jersey Beach). Weiss gatherings centered on religion—weddings, bar and bas mitzvahs, funerals. Until the eighth grade, I went to a parochial school and learned Hebrew, which I can still read to this day.

When I was thirteen, and it was time for my bas mitzvah (a religious ceremony similar to Confirmation in the Christian faith), I studied hard to learn all that I would have to sing and recite at the synagogue. But Solomon the Great—and I never forgave him for this—refused to come because the ceremony was to take place in a conservative synagogue (my father's preference) and not an Orthodox synagogue (my grandfather's). All of this would sour me on religion. I never lost my faith in God, but religion seemed all tied up in family hostility, money, and intolerance of other creeds.

My mother wanted a cultured life for her daughter. She must have loved Shirley Temple, because my hair was permed with the same foul-smelling Tonette perms as was the child star's hair. My room was pretty in pink, from canopied bed to carpet. These were my mother's choices, and she would go on making choices for me—in friends, hobbies, clothes, schools, food. And when it came time to rebel in my teenage years, my targets were close to home. Mother. Religion. Authority.

I yearned for a mother who would teach me to sew, cook, and clean, pick me up after school, and patiently listen to how I could outrun every girl in my class, attend a play with me, explain menstruation to me, talk to me about boys and sex, be a friend. My mother was an absentee mother, with no time for mothering, only work. My father would press her to take time off, but she always refused. One winter he coerced her into vacationing with him in Bermuda—but only by flying there first, calling her on the phone, and coaxing her onto an airplane.

My mother would leave for work early in the morning and return at suppertime, tired after being on her feet all day. Even so, she insisted we always eat as a family. But dinner was either plucked from the freezer or thrown together, and we chided her that we knew the meal was ready when the smoke signals went up.

"What's your favorite thing to make for dinner?" we'd ask her, like one comic feeding a line to another.

"A reservation," she'd reply.

I could never understand why my father was overweight until my teenage years. I would go out on dates and stop in at Holly's Restaurant, a family haunt, for a bite to eat on the way home, and there I was shocked to learn that my father was a regular every evening. Small wonder he ate like a bird at our dinner table. He'd already eaten a proper meal at Holly's!

At home, meanwhile, unyielding mother and spirited daughter clashed. "I'll go to my grave before I let you destroy me!" was her mantra then. Our shouting (and my crying) became routine. She wanted Bach, I wanted bareback. She wanted minuets, I wanted pirouettes. How, she asked, could I be so ungrateful when she was working so hard—for me? Mother Martyr poured on the guilt while making the gelt (Yiddish for money).

All at once my ally, pal, and coconspirator, my father did his best to referee mother-daughter battles—and to make us laugh. Wherever he went, he brought mischief. My mother loved his jokes and pranks (he let one of the girls in the lingerie store know she had bad breath by constantly placing breath mints in her coat pockets).

My father would tell the story of my mother as a young bride washing the kitchen floor—not by getting down on her hands and knees, but by sitting on a chair and moving mop and pail around the room. It was one of my father's set pieces to amuse a crowd, imitating Jene Weiss, the washerwoman with style.

He would also tease my mother when she joined us at Bear Mountain, for example, to ski or tobbagan. She would look stunning in her powder blue ski parka, then ski backward down the bunny slope. While my father was a natural athlete, my mother was a klutz (indeed he called her, with affection, "Gracie," after George Burns's bumbling sidekick Gracie Allen). My mother once tried to christen Dad's newly built boat with a bottle of champagne but missed the target completely and cast the bottle into the drink.

While my father and I danced easily and effortlessly, my mother had two left feet. My father once hired a ballroom dance instructor to give himself and me lessons in the basement—in the cha-cha, the mambo, the fox-trot. He and I would practice while mom did the bookkeeping upstairs. He was a wonderful dance partner, strong in his lead and patient. And while my mother loved to hear me play Chopin's nocturnes or Claude Debussy's "The Children's Corner," my father wanted the Everly Brothers' "Wake Up Little Suzie" or Elvis Presley's "Blue Suede Shoes." He and I would dance to Chubby Checker's "Twist" until he either threw out his back or I collapsed from laughter at his antics.

But despite all his efforts, mother and daughter skirmished more and more. I wanted my mother's attention, and I did things to get it. When I was thirteen, I tore off all the labels on cans in her pantry so she wouldn't know what she was opening. Apprehended while smoking in the bathroom *(verboten),* I tossed the match into a toilet full of toilet paper and managed to set the seat on fire. I refused to eat my mother's cooking. I made Jell-O in the bathtub. I dropped the Ann from my name to defy my mother, who had insisted I be called by the refined name of Carole Ann, not plain old Carole. I had, or so I was told, musical talent. But I refused to practice piano, and finally my Juilliard teacher quit in disgust.

At sixteen, I'd taken a spill off a horse and fractured my left leg. On crutches, I was given a key to the high school elevator—reserved for staff and the disabled—so I wouldn't have to climb the three flights of stairs at Teaneck High School. Possessed of an entrepreneurial spirit, I had a hundred copies of the key made and sold them to willing customers at $5 a pop. My scheme was soon discovered, and my mother was called into the principal's office. For my punishment, I did community service as a candy striper at Holy Name Hospital and returned my ill-gotten gains as a donation to the school library.

Soon enough I became a hit with the bad crowd—boys who wore their hair like Elvis, girls who wore tight black sweaters, short skirts, and lots of makeup. I didn't fit in, but I liked the idea of being a rebel. (Down the road I would be drawn to the beat poetry of Lenny Bruce, the jazz of Dave Brubeck and Miles Davis, concerts at the Apollo in Harlem, and dark little nightclubs in Greenwich Village.)

My mother tried to stop me dating boys she didn't approve of because they were gentile or from the wrong side of the tracks. I would duck that dictum by secretly meeting a boy at the dance or sneak out of the house and not tell her where I had been. I mightily resented my mother's dictatorial manner, and—I am ashamed to admit this now—I mocked her in terrible ways. "Heil Jene!" I would say, which of course put her into a lather.

When I was fifteen, confident and even cocksure, I went joyriding one night in the family car. The fact that I had no license or even a learner's permit seemed not to matter. I had been talking on the phone to a girlfriend who lived a few miles away. My parents were out for the evening, and the Bonneville in the garage was simply too tempting. I made it to my friend's house without incident, but on the way home a policeman pulled me over. My face flushed, heart pounding, I anticipated a night in jail. But the policeman only asked that I dim my bright lights before rushing off to another call, leaving me to fumble for the switch. I never did locate it; I drove the rest of the way home with the brights on, shut the car off in the garage, and breathed a sigh of relief before reporting my adventure to my girlfriend. I called it my Bright Lights, Dim Wit story, and never divulged it to my parents.

Eventually I saved up enough money to buy my own car, a sensible old Ford Falcon. But in my twenties, my taste in cars changed. I would come to admire fast and antique cars, culminating in the 1953 bathtub-style Porsche Super Coupe that would factor in the defining moment of my life. But before that there were Corvettes, an MGTD, an Austin-Healey, a Mercedes, a Karmann Ghia, an MG Midget. I was smitten with speed and living close to the edge. I loved the rush of taking a quick corner in one of those cars, or on my Yamaha 125 dirt bike. I even dated a man who competed on the pro circuit. In the show ring, a similar thrill came from my palomino quarter horse. I was young and thought myself invincible.

I liked being a little out of control, and my mother was all about control, so I did what I thought I had to do to escape her clutches. At the age of eighteen, I married an accountant, just to get out of the house. The marriage was annulled several months later. Three years down the road, I did it again, marrying a teacher. That marriage lasted three years. Both weddings were lavish, with my mother pulling all the strings.

I couldn't pick a mate to save my life, yet I had much to be thankful for. By my mid-twenties, I had a master's degree in multicultural education, an abiding interest in diverse languages and cultures, and a teaching job at Washington Elementary School in Union City, New Jersey—"little Havana," as they called it, because of all the Cuban émigrés who lived there.

I loved being in a classroom, teaching Spanish children to learn English. I would take them to supermarkets, and they would learn to shop in their new language. Later they would bring their parents and pass on what they had learned. The beauty of teaching children, I soon learned, is that kids have no inhibitions about language. Mine was gratifying work.

I was also studying for a doctoral degree in education. I had an active social life and a boyfriend, Don Goldman, a sweet and fun-loving man.

I was a natural athlete, and my body was trim and shapely, kept so by riding, workouts, and even belly-dancing classes. I wore clothes that showed that body off—two-piece bathing suits, short shorts, halter tops, sundresses. I was, to use the parlance of the day, "a fox." I turned heads, both men's and women's. The wolf whistles told me that I was admired, and I liked the feeling. It did wonders for my ego and self-esteem.

And my skin. It was flawless. Like porcelain. Never a pimple, no birthmark, not one blemish. Skin as smooth and soft as a baby's.

*　　*　　*

I also, and finally, had my own horse.

It took a while to acquire him. My mother had promised me I

could have one when I was old enough to afford my own. All in due time. Due time came in my mid-twenties, when my "horse account" had grown fat enough and I could also afford my own place.

The first horse I would ever call mine was a quiet palomino quarter horse named Bailey, for the Irish Cream color of his coat. Of a medium gold (Trigger's color) and standing about 15.1 hands high, he had a white star on his forehead that seemed to lend him a little class. He was blocky, with short ears, and wide between the eyes—a trait I've always looked for in a horse, as it suggests a sizable brain behind it. Bailey had large, liquid, dark eyes—a kind eye, as horse people say. He had a long neck and a powerful chest and shoulders, and, like his ancestors, he was built for sprinting short distances (the quarter horse was bred specifically to run the quarter-mile, thus the name) or turning a wandering cow back to the herd.

I had heard that at Mar-Bel's, a nearby stable in Montvale, New Jersey, a boarder was moving and aiming to sell her horse. He had been a pleasure horse and a school horse, and had competed at local shows. Ridden both English and western, Bailey was by then fifteen years old.

I was told that his registration papers had been lost, but his owner said she traced his line back to the foundation quarter horse sire Joe Bailey. Laid-back and seasoned, he seemed the right size for me and the right disposition for a first-time horse owner. I had been around stables enough to know that green riders and green horses make for a bad combination. There is an old saying among horse people: "Green on green make black and blue."

I wanted a horse who would build up my confidence. I could see Bailey was an honest trooper, patient and good-natured. I watched him being ridden and lunged, and one day I tried him out myself. When I got on, he turned his head, fixed his calm, dark eyes on me, and sniffed at my stirrups, as if to check me out. I immediately felt at ease on his back, and was impressed by his blend of willingness and submission. Right away, I could tell that this was the beginning of a beautiful friendship. Here was a horse I'd be able to experiment on, even ride bareback. If I made mistakes, it wouldn't matter. He was that forgiving. Then, as if to seal the deal, when I was back on the ground he started licking my hands and face. I couldn't resist Bailey.

I kept him at Mar-Bel's Stable and rode him several times a week. My passion for horses had faded just a little, for horses had to compete with all the other demands on my time—job, boyfriend, cars. I could not have predicted what role horses would play in my life, the version that unfolded after November 22, 1975.

3

Blue Flame

ON NOVEMBER 22, 1975, my vocabulary would change. Mundane words such as *lesson plan, morning traffic, boyfriend,* and *tennis club* would in an instant give way to medical terms such as *skin graft, debride, burn unit, burn victim.*

I remember everything about that day, at least leading up to the fire. The weather: damp and dreary. The headlines in the morning paper: John F. Kennedy had been assassinated in Dallas that same day twelve years beforehand. I can tell you what I wore at breakfast that morning in my little rented house in River Edge, New Jersey: a blue terry-cloth robe that had started to fray. I remember my dog December—a little black-and-white cockerpoo named for the month I got her—following closely at my heels as she always did, and the *tic-tic-tic* of her nails on the vinyl floor. I remember sipping freshly brewed *café con leche,* and the sense of anticipation that marked the day.

It was too raw and wet to ride Bailey; I would ride him tomorrow, I told myself, and hope for better weather. Still, it was a day off. No school, no morning traffic to fight, no parking space to find, no lesson plans to review. I would instead do something I had been putting off: work on my car, the '53 Porsche Super Coupe, lying dismantled in the basement. Nick, a friend who was also a mechanic, had previously disassembled the engine to allow for repairs.

I remember what I wore to the task. Faded jeans. Yellow sweater. Sneakers. I remember putting on a jacket and driving my MG Midget to a nearby gas station to fill up a gas can, for my first task was to use gasoline to clean engine parts, as Nick had instructed me. (In hindsight, he should have suggested I use kerosene, which is less flammable, or better, parts cleaner. As a mechanic in a garage, Nick should have known better, but he presumed I'd be working outside. And I would have, had the weather been kinder. He would wait for more than a year and a half after the fire before visiting me; I took it as a sign of guilt.)

I had poured gasoline into a paint tray and was holding a gas-soaked rag in my left hand, accompanying Linda Ronstadt as she sang "Desperado" on my tape player, when in walked Nick, a slender young man in his twenties, wearing his blue Chevy dealer coveralls, his head of thick, dark hair all tousled.

"I'm way ahead of you," I told him. I was kneeling in one corner of the room, the five-gallon gas can next to me on the floor. "I've already started." I held up the rag for him to see. "I'm cleaning the parts you laid out."

As Nick started to gather his tools, there was another knock at the basement door. It was my boyfriend, Don, his long red hair touching the top of his sweatshirt. Though not mechanically inclined, he loved that broken Porsche as much as I did and wanted to see it back on the road.

"What can I do, Nick?" he asked, then added, "You can give Carole the messy jobs."

That was the last thing I remember before blue flame streaked across the floor and turned my kneeling form into a human torch. I remember a loud *whooooomp,* followed by unbearable heat and light. Still kneeling, the position of prayer, I threw one hand up over my eyes to shield against the brightness and with the other tried desperately to put out the flames. Pain hit me like a train, and my entire body reeled in agony from the heat. I tried to scream, but no sound would come.

I heard Don's frantic plea to Nick to call the police and fire department, and Nick must have rushed upstairs to do just that. Finally, I managed three words. "Save yourself, Don!" I cried.

As quickly as he could—how much time had elapsed? Twenty seconds? Thirty? One minute? Two?—Don found an old braided rug, wrapped me in it, and used his hands to put out the small fires that still flared. He carried me upstairs and outside, onto the porch. By now shock had set in, and things got blurry. But I do remember looking into Don's face. It was the most frightened face I had ever seen in my life.

Scorched flesh immediately begins to expand. This is part of the physics of fire, as I would later come to understand. My clothes had melted and fused to my body, and I experienced a growing tightness around my waist and upper legs. My whole body was swelling. At one point, I put a finger to my face, and it stuck to the melted flesh that had once been my lower lip. When I pulled my finger free, the lip followed, like melted wax.

An ambulance came and whisked me to Hackensack Hospital, just minutes away. The emergency medical technician, I later learned, had immediately started an intravenous line to get fluids and pain medication into me. I remember the wail of the siren, the rotating lights, Don at my side never losing that look of pure terror. I recall being whirled into an operating room. Then darkness.

❖　　❖　　❖

We do not so much remember events in our past as the memory of them. We have memories of memories. Not long ago a friend had sent me a copy of an award-winning essay by Jonathan Franzen in the *New Yorker* called "My Father's Brain." The article was subtitled "What Alzheimer's Takes Away," and though the piece was intensely personal, it also included some fascinating detail on how memory works, or at least current thinking on the matter.

It seems we have the ability to forget almost everything that has ever happened to us. The few specific memories that we do retain get hard-wired into the brain, becoming what Franzen calls "part of the architecture of the brain" as we visit and revisit those memories.

These are my memories of that first lifesaving surgery, memories that will remain part of the architecture of my brain until the day I die. A man was holding my hand under glaring lights.

"Carole, can you hear me? I'm holding your hand. If you can hear me, squeeze."

And I did as he asked.

"Okay," the man said, "one squeeze will mean yes and two means no." He continued, "Your body took a horrible shock. I have to do surgery on you. Can you handle this?" And I squeezed his hand for yes before sinking into more darkness.

The man, I later learned, was Dr. Anthony Barbara, and he would spend six grueling hours cutting off the clothes that had fused to my skin, and scraping away roasted black flesh from my body.

*　　＊　　＊*

My mother has her own memories of that day. She remembers, acutely, conversations that took place—on that day and afterward—between her and doctors, her and relatives, her and her daughter lying in a hospital bed. She is the star witness to the most gruesome event in both our lives. Many years after the accident, I recorded my mother's memories on a cassette tape, to keep those memories alive.

"It was the Saturday before Thanksgiving," my mother remembers. My father was away on the coast, moving his boat from New Jersey to Florida. He was hoping to start up a charter fishing business down there, the same sort of thing he had done when he was younger. He would call my mother from phone booths in every port. "I'm fine," he'd say, "everything okay there?" But he had poor hearing and would never hear what my mother said; he'd hang up and then call again from the next place.

That Saturday, my mother got a call at the store in Bergen Mall at about four o'clock. The Hackensack police told her that her daughter had been in an accident, that she was badly burned and had been taken in an ambulance to Hackensack Hospital.

My mother announced to the crowded store that she had an

emergency, and they had to leave *immediately*. Her sister, Rose, who was working with her that day, insisted on accompanying my mother, and they somehow found their way to the hospital.

Breathless when she got there, my mother demanded to know my condition. Someone well used to frantic relatives, even imperious ones, told her to sit down. "Your daughter," the clerk told her, "is in surgery." And there they sat, the two sisters, alternating for hours between tears and hysteria, sitting, then pacing, my mother eventually collecting herself enough to call burn centers in New York, Boston, and Texas. Finally, at ten-thirty that night, my mother was led into a room alone.

My mother remembers a lot of beds, and people lying on stretchers. She was looking for me, but I spotted her first.

"Mommy, it's me," I said. "I'm here."

It was my voice, but I was, my mother recalls, beyond recognition. "Your skin," she would later say, "was red, your face was swollen, your lips were huge and projected. Your head was the size of a pumpkin, a very big pumpkin. I had passed you right by. The voice alone, though faint and little, was the same. You were crying, and the tears were coming down. The attendant then came along and said not to make you talk, that you were too weak to speak. Then they wheeled you away. I couldn't hold your hand because you were wrapped like a mummy, with just two fingers of your right hand showing."

My mother remembers an aide readjusting my cap above my ear. I had said it was too tight. She later remarked on how everything in that room was a pale green, pea green—the doctors' uniforms, the walls.

"They were all," she said, "that awful color. I disliked green for a long time after that."

※　　　❀　　　✦

When next I awoke, my throat was parched. I was alone in a hospital room, and I could see darkness through the window. Though I was in a morphine stupor, I was conscious enough to see my mother at my bedside. When I saw the expression on her face, I thought back to Don's face in the ambulance. The look of devastation was the same, and the effect on me was the same. I was reminded once more.

It's that bad.

The room was hot, unbearably hot. I couldn't move, for I was wrapped in bandages head to toe, wires entering me from everywhere. The hospital bed had its sides up, to prevent me from rolling off. Fat chance.

I could only look up and see the slow, constant drip of an IV bottle hung upside down on a stand, its fluid running through tubes and into my right arm. I could feel another tube, a catheter, under my leg. Tubes in, tubes out; fluid in, fluid out.

The walls were pale yellow, and near me, on a stand, was a portable gray tray with an untouched cup of water and several straws. I wanted water, needed water. So close, yet so far. If I called out for a drink, no one could hear me. The door was closed. Finally it opened. Figures were coming in and out of the room, dressed in white. The sheets, too, were white and crisp. And I was black, cooked beyond recognition.

When the door opened, I saw a sign that read, "Isolation: Do

Not Enter." So. I was in solitary confinement, imprisoned in my own lifeless body, unable to turn off my mind.

The screams from neighboring patients in the burn unit were piercing. I couldn't make out the whispers of the nurses talking to my mother. Even my mother was hard to recognize: she wore a blue disposable paper gown, hat, and mask. Her hands were wringing tissues, and one after another drop to the floor. Like sorrowful rain.

God was punishing me, I thought. Perhaps I deserved the punishment. This room already smelled of death, my death. The stench of rotten flesh, my flesh, was everywhere, like the smell of hair burning, only far worse. It was a smell to bring up one's guts, a smell I will never, ever forget.

I hoped to God this was only a nightmare. I called out for more morphine. Anything to escape this hell. I am afraid of needles, but this one I really wanted. As the drug kicked in, I felt a warm rush, and the radio in my head offered the chorus of a favorite gospel tune.

> Oh come, angel band
> Come and around me stand
> Oh bear me away on your snow-white wings
> to my eternal home.
> Oh bear me away on your snow-white wings
> to my eternal home.

These nurses in white uniforms, I thought, must be the angels coming for me. Merciful, merciful morphine. It lured me back into a dark and ever silent sleep.

After the first surgery, my mother met the doctor who had operated on me. It would have been evening by now, surely the longest day in my mother's long life. By then Dr. Barbara had dispensed with the green hospital scrubs and reappeared in his office in a three-piece navy blue suit. With his Italian blood, dark hair, and bright eyes, he reminded my mother of Tony Bennett. Dr. Barbara looked dapper but exhausted from the marathon surgery.

My mother unleashed a salvo of questions, sometimes giving him no chance to answer.

"Do you have a prognosis for my daughter?" then, before he could answer, "I'll tell you right now, I want my daughter alive. I want her to live! I'll take her to the ends of the world to see that she lives. I've called every burn center in the country, and Boston is ready to airlift her there to their burn center."

Inclined to be a little stiff, Dr. Barbara was apparently blunt and calm in his reply. "The end of her world," he told her, "may be right here."

"What are you talking about?"

"Mrs. Rosenberg, I'll give it to you straight. Your daughter has second- and third-degree burns over sixty-five percent of her body. Those burns are horribly deep. You'll be very lucky if your daughter makes it through the night. Her life now is hanging by a thread. And if she makes it through the night, at eight o'clock tomorrow morning, she'll go in for more surgery."

Dr. Barbara patiently began to educate my mother in how human skin reacts to fire. How the body swells, how the burned skin becomes a haven for infections, how that skin must therefore be continually debrided—literally scrubbed clean. How healthy skin protects the body and how a body deprived of such protection is prey to infections ("roaring infections," he called them) and high fever. How absolute sterility is a must. How new skin has to be harvested from unscathed parts of the body (in my case, only the back, upper chest, stomach, and right arm) and grafted onto sections that have been scorched.

There was more. The swelling of the burn victim's body limits blood flow to the extremities, and such swelling can only be relieved by surgically cutting "releases" in the tightening skin. My burns were both second and third degree. The former involves damage to the outer layer of skin (the epidermis) and the underlying dermis; the latter involves damage to all three layers of skin—epidermis, dermis, and hypodermis—and often destroys underlying fat, muscle, nerve, and bone tissue.

Gasoline fumes, I came to learn, are four times heavier than air, so all those fumes would have gathered around me as I knelt by the paint tray and the gas can. Kneeling made everything worse. The radiant heat alone from a gas explosion generates 1,000-degree-Fahrenheit heat, twice as hot as any kitchen oven. Then there was the heat of the flames, at 1,500 degrees, and I was their epicenter.

The gas explosion—whose cause I would not discover until years later—had destroyed not only much of my skin but also, to a great extent, muscle in both my legs and feet, my buttocks, my diaphragm, my left arm and hand, and the lower part of my face. All of this put me in a high-risk medical category with a survival rate of less than 10 percent.

"If she survives," Dr. Barbara told my mother, "it's very likely she'll never walk again. And the excruciating pain she'll face could affect her mind. She could become a vegetable."

"Doctor, I'm going to tell you something." My mother, I know, would have set her jaw as she said these words in Dr. Barbara's office. "My daughter is going to live. You're not going in there alone tomorrow. I'm sending you in there with God. Don't you forget for one second that God will be with you. It's up to you."

Dr. Barbara could not believe what he was hearing. "Mrs. Rosenberg," he said, "we've never met before. And you're putting the whole responsibility of your daughter's life in my hands? You know, the smallest surgical procedure can be a gamble. I know what you're saying. But I am not an executioner, I'm a doctor. I will do everything in my power to make your daughter survive. But if she lives, you'll have a long, hard row to hoe ahead of you."

That would prove an understatement.

Of the five brothers and sisters in the Weiss family, Jennie is the only one with fair hair and midnight blue eyes. She longed for a child with blue eyes, fair and blond, and she got her wish. My blue eyes, thanks to my father, were even bluer than my mother's. And now that precious daughter seemed perilously close to dying. A certain kind of mother would have cracked under the strain. Not Jennie Rosenberg.

That night there was a family meeting at our house in Teaneck. My mother remembers that Uncle Herbie was crying a river, that Aunt Rose was hysterical. My mother also cried, but she was never hysterical. Every movement, she told herself, had to be well thought out. She remembers, acutely, the need to be alone, to clear her head, to have a plan. In that moment, she took charge.

She instructed her brother to go home, get some sleep, and in the morning, start saying *tillum,* a prayer for a loved one in mortal danger. She advised her sister to do the same. My father, somewhere on the coast, was still calling home regularly from this or that port, but it was strictly one-way communication, meant to assure my mother that all was well with him. But all was not well with her, and scream as she might into the telephone, he could not hear what my mother was saying. She would face this ordeal alone.

Though not exactly alone. My mother is no mystic, but that night around two o'clock, as she lay exhausted on the bed, weak from crying but empty of tears and unable to sleep, her father appeared to her in a vision. Nothing like this had ever happened to her before, and nothing like it has happened since.

Solomon Weiss called her by her Jewish name, Yached. Pronounced *yalk*-ed, it means "the one and only." "Don't cry anymore," he told her. "Roll up your sleeves and get to work. Carole needs your strength, not your tears. You be strong, and so will she."

Blue-eyed mother and blue-eyed daughter were about to begin their "long hard row to hoe," and the first few steps would prove the most painful.

4

Death Wish

ON THE DAWN of the morning after the fire, a Sunday, my mother
began a new phase of motherhood. She was about to become my
feeder and caretaker, my intermediary, my dispenser of faith and
hope. She would literally breathe life into me.

Before sunrise, my mother gave me much the same spiritual
coaching as she had given Dr. Barbara. I was in a Demerol-induced
haze, but I remember what she said: "Carole, you're not going in
there alone. You're going in there with God."

The drugs were making my head spin and my body numb. My
lips felt like lead, and words were difficult to form. Visions of
injured and euthanized animals popped crazily into my head.
Surely I was watching a movie of someone else lying in this bed.
Unable to move any part of myself, I felt trapped in my own body.

"Mom, why didn't I die?" I whispered. "I didn't die, but I should
have." It would not be the first time I would express that wish.

"Don't say that!" my mother replied. "Carole, darling, you're going to live. You must remember that—you are going to live and you'll always be beautiful. You'll be beautiful on the inside and the outside. You'll have double beauty. Just *live!*"

Surviving the critical first night and day came down to several factors: my youth, my excellent health, and the fact that there was no smoke inhalation or lung damage to contend with. That, and the skill of the medical team at Hackensack Hospital—Dr. Barbara, an Indian doctor named Dr. Patnaik, and the twenty-six nurses who were assigned to me on a rotating two-hour basis.

Two hours was deemed to be the limit, for my room was kept at ninety degrees to reduce the risk of chills or pneumonia. Mine was the biggest room on the floor, with the most equipment: rotating bed, ice mattresses, and a dome heat lamp over the bed. The nurses on the floor, the fourth, were instructed to medicate me with heavy doses of morphine and Demerol and to feed me when my mother wasn't there. But the heat of the room and the stench of infection must have been hard to bear, for everyone. All the flowers and cards on every flat surface failed to brighten that room.

Around noon on the day following the fire, the team of doctors—including Dr. Barbara and Dr. Patnaik—huddled with my mother. I was still alive, but their news was grim, their forecast bleak.

"The first stage is behind us," Dr. Barbara told her. "If the infections don't kill her, she'll make it. She'll probably not walk, and she'll have no use of her left hand, and she'll have many scars and many skin grafts. This is going to be a lengthy process. We have to wait for the donor sites to heal before we can take more skin, and as you know, there is very little unburned area to take the grafts from. I must be straightforward with you. Not too many patients with these kinds of burns survive this whole ordeal."

Ever direct, my mother asked him, "Are you the best specialist?"

"Probably not," he replied. "But I'm the best you have to deal with. Your daughter won't survive a trip to Boston. It's not even an option. Besides, in Boston she won't have the support of family and friends, which is absolutely critical for her emotional support. Her support is right here. We'll take it day by day. Right now it's hour by hour, then week by week if we go that far. There will be plenty of surgeries and plenty of consequences."

I had never known fear before this time, but I would become intimate with fear. I was afraid of needles, of being anesthetized, of not waking up. I was afraid of not being in control, and there was no one to make the fear go away. That's when I understood unequivocally: though I had the support of family and friends, and often superb medical care, I was ultimately in this alone.

Dr. Barbara had tried to warn my family and me about the pain that lay ahead, for burn units are the epitome of pain. But nothing could have prepared me for debriding. I never thought I would survive that first debriding.

The nurses wheeled me down the corridor to a T intersection and from there into the tank room. They laid me on a flat gurney, which was lowered into an oval metal tank (a so-called Hubbard tank) of warm water and Betadine. Several nurses held my arms and legs while others scrubbed my wounds with gauze. I writhed to get free, and as much as I tried to stifle my own screams, it was impossible. I thought I'd pass out from the pain.

Have you ever put iodine on a wound and felt the sting? That's how my whole body felt. As if so many hornets were eating away at my flesh. I was crying, tears streaming down my face, screaming for them to stop. I did not swear; that's not my style. But I did scream. "Get me out of here! I wanna die! Please, just let me die! Don't touch me. No more. I can't stand it!" I thought I would go out of my mind.

Then they gave me more morphine and Demerol. When they carried me back to my bed, I was virtually lifeless. The pain resonated for hours. Every day of my first month in the hospital, I faced a debriding session that lasted twenty minutes—but I had never known minutes like that. I dreaded those sessions, and no amount of morphine could make a dent in the pain. Later, the debriding schedule was modified to four times a week, but the treatments were still hellish. Long after I left the hospital, I would wash my own skin and be oh so gentle with the washcloth, ever so light with my hands, as if to console my skin for all the abuse it had taken.

One nurse at Hackensack stood out from them all. Her name was Toni Kardell, and she always spoke gently to me. There was a fresh scent about her, like clean laundry hung outside to dry. She understood the relationship I had with my mother, and she often counseled me, as a friend would. But she was more than a friend; she was an angel.

Antonia Kardell was thirty-something, trim, medium height

with short blond hair, very pretty, refined, and elegant, wise beyond her years. She had a Dutch accent, a throaty voice, a gentle touch, and the sunniest disposition, always encouraging but still acknowledging the patient's pain. Toni had the gift of inner radar, the ability to understand what someone else was feeling. She was a nurturer by nature.

And she made me laugh, which helped temper the pain. In a show of solidarity, she would drink through a straw, as I was forced to do because of my turned-down lip. Or she would put a turban or scarf on her head to show me what I would look like wearing one. She spent hours with me, listening to me, reading to me, explaining all the procedures I would have to endure, telling me how brave I was. I asked if she could be my private nurse; that's how much I liked her.

But even an angel cannot defeat the blackness that a burn victim faces, knowing that this is home, this is life, for months and months to come. People who spend extended periods in hospital often say that major procedures, such as surgery, are less of a burden: at least they knock you out for those. It's the constant little interventions that make you feel as if you're being eaten alive.

Tubes were inserted into me—one to feed me intravenously, a catheter to eliminate the problem of urination. I was stuck with needles constantly, for pain medication, for blood work, for sleep, as a precursor to feeding. (The irony was that I was, and remain, terrified of needles.) You would think there would be some peace in a hospital. Not so. Hackensack Hospital was quiet, even somber—save for patients screaming, either from pain or for painkiller. But nurses and orderlies were always doing something to me. Always, even at night.

Night nurses would come and give me medication or check on one thing or another. Change IVs, change sheets and beds and mattresses, empty bedpans, give needles, take bandages off or put new ones on, make me drink fluids, administer therapy, on and on.

And every inch of burned skin had to be replaced with fresh skin taken from elsewhere on my body. Today, doctors can take an area of skin no bigger than a postage stamp and grow it, like culture in a medium. In three weeks, enough new skin can be grown to cover the entire body, thus speeding up the grafting process and shortening the stay in hospital. But in those days, it was a straight exchange—new skin for damaged skin. Doctors would take skin from my stomach or back and use it on my burned legs. They used a tool similar to a wood planer, with a sharp blade that shaved off the top layer of skin (.012 of an inch deep), several inches at a time. The skin grafts caused pain that was almost as bad as the burns themselves, and once the donor site was healed, the doctors would go back for more. I was constantly being wrapped and unwrapped, like the body of some dead Egyptian queen the burial bureaucrats kept fussing over, trying to get the bandages just right.

※　　　◆　　　※

A day after the accident, my family gathered at the house in Teaneck. My mother remembers that they got a dinner from a kosher deli, but nobody could eat. They were too overwrought, all of them crying. Worst, she recalls, were the phone calls from friends and relations. My mother would tell my story over and over, until finally she could bear it no longer.

"People," she told them when they called, "you'll have to get it from the grapevine. It's ripping out another piece of my heart. I can't repeat it over and over again."

Three days had passed, and still my father remained blissfully unaware of his daughter's fate. Finally, on Tuesday, my mother heard from my father at their Florida condominium, where a telephone fitted with a microphone enabled a proper connection. He swallowed the terrible news, got on a plane, and rushed to my side.

My mother recalls him coming home after he had seen me in hospital. She had never seen a man break down like that. He got hysterical and kept on repeating "Not Carole, not my Channala" (my Hebrew name, pronounced *Hah*-nala). As she would do throughout this ordeal, my mother took charge.

She was direct with him, and she remembers saying, "Irving, I don't need a second casualty. Turn the faucet off. How can I help her if I have to help you? Every bit that I help you, I help her less."

My mother believed at that moment she had gotten through to my father, had penetrated his grief and called on his inner resources. But she hadn't, not really. Every other night, she recalls, he would cry out in his sleep, "Not Carole, not my Channala! I have one daughter! Not her, no, no!" In the morning he would tell his wife, "My brain isn't crying. It's my heart. My heart cries."

My mother, as I have said, gave me life twice. On Thanksgiving Day, just five days after the fire, my family—my father, mother, and brother, along with my boyfriend Don—gathered in my room. My food tray (it was blue plastic, with small compartments, the kind of thing you see in the military or jail) lay untouched. That night I was hit with a high fever, the thing that burn victims are prone to, and that Dr. Barbara had warned about. And nothing would bring down my body temperature, which soared to 104 degrees. For two days I was positioned between two rubber ice mattresses and hooked up to a machine that would chill my body. The nurses placed cold, wet towels on my forehead and under my arms while administering fluids. There was no escape from this "meat locker" that caused me to shiver and shake.

When the fever continued unabated into a third night, my mother came to the hospital, and a nurse told her to call the rabbi for the last rites. "She's going to convulse," she remembers a nurse telling her.

My mother then held my tongue so I wouldn't choke on it. But I said nothing, she recalls; my eyes were almost closed, and I was not responding.

"Carole," she remembers telling me, "please don't leave me now. Please cooperate." Then she breathed into my mouth and gave me artificial respiration.

"Let's say the *shmah*," she then said. It's a prayer made on waking and sleeping, offering thanks for the day and hope for another.

"Shmah Israel, Hear O Israel, the Lord, Our God . . . Say it after me," she told me, and she moved my lips until they started to move on their own.

There was a chair in the corner. My mother says she slept there all night. Minute by minute I came back. The ice packs were removed, and my temperature dropped. They took me off the ice mattress.

"Talk," my mother said to me, "talk." She was afraid that if I fell asleep, I would never wake.

I remember telling my mother, "I'll never forget this as long as I live. Mom, I love you so much, you and Dad and Michael. Everyone has been so marvelous to me. But you, Mom, I owe you one. Someday I'll repay you for everything you've done. I want you to have your *naches*" (pronounced *NA*-hess, it's Yiddish for "good cheer, good fortune").

"If you live," my mother replied, "that'll be my *naches*."

The doctor came in that morning. "It's a miracle," he told my mother. "These things never happen."

My mother kept saying how determined I was, what a fighter I was, how I hadn't survived this for nothing. "It'll be for something," she kept telling me. "It's got to be for something."

Here was a mother managing to keep herself collected with her daughter close to dying. Her sheer will and drive kept me alive. I remember lying in that hospital bed with roaring infections, and she would rub my throat and try to get fluids into me. "Never say die," she kept repeating. I've never known anyone with as much tenacity.

❖   ❄   ❖

After a month of enduring medical procedures, I came to certain conclusions. Hackensack Hospital was a numbers game, and I knew my numbers well. Temperature in my room: 90 degrees. My body temperature: 100.2 degrees. My weight before the fire: 100 pounds. My weight a month after the fire: 68 pounds. Millimeters of morphine in my IV drip: 4. Number of nurses on my case: 26.

"Twenty-six nurses," my mother recalls, "twenty-six headaches." Some were rough, some rigid, some were soft and easy. They came in all ages, shapes, and sizes, and each had a different personality. The one nurse my mother remembered most fondly was, of course, Toni Kardell; she was, as Dad called her, "a Dutch treat."

All the nurses had been instructed to ensure that nothing metal be allowed in my room, lest I see my own reflection or harm myself. All mirrors were removed, and my eating utensils were plastic. One of the nurses was a massive and dowdy young woman named Ruth. My age, she had skin scarred by acne and possessed the strength of two nurses. I dreaded seeing her and often asked that someone else tend to me. I saw her glacial side and, even in my hideous condition, her jealousy of me.

On Christmas Day, 1975, the dreaded debriding ritual was especially excruciating, for the nurse on duty that day was the dreaded Ruth. Ruthless, I had dubbed her. She was built like a heavyweight boxer, and everything about her was heavy, heavy hands, heavy heart—if she had any heart at all, for she owned a dispassionate face. I knew that nurses employed in this job—debriding, working in a burn unit—had to be emotionally distant. But there was no pleasantness in Ruth at all. Just bitterness. She was my least favorite nurse because she handled me like a slab of meat, and worse, she was cranky this day.

I was in no mood to be roughed up. As she scrubbed me, I pressed my lips together hard. Repressing a piercing scream was so tough, so painful. I clenched my hand so hard, my nails hurt my palm. "C'mon, now," she said, "let me get through with this so I can go to lunch."

"The hell you will!" I came back. With my free hand, I tossed the tray, the needles, and all their contents across the room.

Ruth turned red with anger. Her glare was like a dagger that cut through me. "You spoiled rotten brat," she said. "You think with all your family's money and your boat, that you're better than me? You're stuck with me, kiddo, whether you like it or not."

The day before, my father had shown photos to the nurses and to Dr. Barbara, who liked to fish. One photo showed me in a two-piece bathing suit on the ladder of the flybridge. He wanted to remind me of happier times. But his reminder only served to accentuate what I had lost, and now Ruth had thrown the photo in my face.

For the rest of my time with Ruth that day, I stayed silent. I would not give this malicious creature the satisfaction that her words had wounded me. I was feeling so many emotions then: sadness, depression, anger. (I was not always proud of how I behaved in hospital. One time, an aide was sent in to start an IV. My veins were not easy to see, and she stabbed and stabbed, trying to find one. I called her every name in the book, demanding someone more competent. Finally they sent in a male nurse, but they had to sedate me heavily because I put up such a fuss. No one escaped my wrath, but I was mad at myself, too, for causing everyone else so much bother.)

Later on that day, Ruth cast me an utterly contemptuous look, held out a mirror, and said, "You might as well face yourself." More than likely, she was getting revenge for the tray incident. The face staring back at me reminded me of a scary Halloween mask. It was far worse than I had imagined.

I looked like some alien creature, or a circus sideshow freak. What I saw in the mirror that day was the kind of image the tabloids showed from time to time. No amount of surgery, I thought, could fix that face.

That moment was one of the darkest of the whole experience. I sank deeper and deeper into a pit. That night, I asked a nurse to write in my journal a poem I dictated to her, a poem called "Looking-Glass."

It went, in part,

Look at yourself,
Take a good long look . . .
We plain Janes of the world
suffer our wrappings.

My eyes brimming wth tears, I later told my father that I was useless. "They put suffering animals down," I said. "Why not me?"

The mirror did not lie. Even my own father considered me with a look of repulsion mixed with compassion. I knew I would be repulsive to any man. All my hopes were swallowed up in darkness. I'd heard the whispers—that my legs were so badly burned I might never walk again. My parents would be burdened with an invalid, and I didn't know if I could face the months and years of pain that lay ahead of me.

My mother remembers how devastated I was. They called her in, and she found me crying. I asked the nurse to leave the room so I could speak to my mother privately.

"You know, Mom," I told her, "you should have let me die. I'm a twisted pretzel of a woman. I can't live like this. Why didn't you just let me die?"

Toni Kardell, who was in charge of all the nurses, then came in. "You know," she told me, "I know you think this is a setback, but you'll have to turn it into a blessing in disguise." Then Toni turned to my mother and said the whole place was in an uproar over the mirror incident. My mother would have to speak with Dr. Barbara—"a tough cookie," as she put it. My mother remembers their conversation quite vividly.

"Here I am again," she recalls saying to him, almost coyly. "Little old me. You have me to deal with." Then the tone in her story changes. "I want the name of the nurse who handed Carole that mirror!"

"I have the name," Dr. Barbara told her. "In fact, there were two nurses involved. How badly do you want those names?"

"I want them fired—*now!*" my mother apparently told him. My mother was furious as she recounted this exchange, as no doubt she was at the time.

"Before I fire her," Dr. Barbara replied, "I want you to listen to reason. You're having a hard time with your daughter. They're having a harder time. The twenty-six nurses are having a harder time with your daughter than she's having with the twenty-six nurses."

And he went over ground that must have been familiar to my mother—their working conditions, the heat in the room, the ripe smell of infection, one very feisty patient.

"If I fire two nurses," Dr. Barbara told my mother, "you'll have twenty-six enemies. You need twenty-six friends for your daughter's well-being. So let's make sure we keep the twenty-six as friends. We may weed one out later, but not now."

My mother had no sympathy for Ruth, but she had plenty for the other nurses. "You were no easy mark," she told me later. "You were the most challenging patient there. There were so many incidents. Every other day my mother would get a call from the hospital. One time Toni Kardell called my mother. "Please come," she said. "We need your help. Your daughter is incorrigible."

When my mother arrived, she found me sitting in the debriding room at the edge of the Hoyer lift and about to be inserted into the chemical tank. I was refusing the medication they wanted to give me. Every time a nurse went to give me painkiller, I wanted to know the dose. If it was 200 cc, I wanted 100. If it was 100, I wanted 50. And I had my reasons.

Across from my room in the hospital was a young woman who had been badly burned during a Halloween party when her bunny-rabbit costume caught on fire. My age, she could not tolerate the pain and got hooked on painkillers. I could hear her moaning in the night, "Give it to me, give it to me," and I was determined not to end up like that. If I became addicted to morphine, I'd have nothing left to fight with.

"I won't blow my mind," I told all who would listen. "It's the only thing I have left."

But some days my mind was not to be trusted. One day I awoke from a drug-induced stupor to find my feet suspended in the air, in traction, with metal plates and pins drilled through them. "They've got me in dancing shoes," I slurred. "I'm dancing . . ." The drugs were playing tricks on my mind, had me convinced those feet weren't mine at all but sides of beef hanging on hooks in a cold meat locker. I'd look up from my pillow at my suspended feet with the metal rods through them and think of Jesus on the cross. I would yearn for the respite of unconsciousness.

5

"He Will Carry You"

HOURS BECAME DAYS, days became weeks, and weeks turned into months. Gone were freedom, mobility, health, beauty, dignity, pride. What I had, in spades, was time. And time had slowed to a crawl.

I kept a journal, wrote poetry, tried to fathom what had happened. That process—of putting pen to paper to get at meaning—would lead, ultimately, to this book. One poem, called "From the Mouth of the Phoenix," refers to my "Demerol dreams," my "sterile kingdom," and my body as "a patchwork quilt." I wrote of my "tiny whimpering voice . . . calling for its mother" and I lamented my "charred body, scraped of its blackness like toast too well done." My questions in that poem were metaphysical ones:

> *God, don't you hear me?*
> *I've incurred the wrath of the almighty. Why me?*
> *Do I want to make it through another day?*
> *God, I promise to be good,*
> *if only you make this a dream.*

I had asked a nurse in my room to write these words down as I dictated them on New Year's Eve, 1975. It had been thirty-eight days since the fire. My mother read the poem and grew desperate. Her promise—"You'll be more beautiful on the inside *and* the outside"—was having no effect. I wasn't buying it, not then. The mirror episode was too fresh. I knew that every magazine ad and television commercial featured glamorous women, and that society judged you by your looks. Appearance, plain and simple, was all that counted.

I was bedridden, hospitalized, imprisoned. And only a month into my sentence, I was not at all sure that I had the fortitude to stomach it to the end, for the end was nowhere in sight. When the hell, I thought, am I going to get out of here? When will it be my turn to leave? When? When?

No one could say. I would see other patients come and go while I remained—confined, indoors, crippled. I hated to have others wash me, feed me, brush my teeth, wipe my bottom. I resented their intimacy with my body. Daily, my privacy and body were violated (or so I thought), and I—who had been living alone, a fiercely independent woman—was now unable to do anything myself.

*   *   *

My jail cell, as I called it, was a room fourteen feet by eighteen feet, with a bathroom and a shower. The room overlooked the parking lot, and my visitors would say they could see trees and cars below. The walls of the room had been painted yellow, a color meant to cheer. The color of the sun. There were some 1,232 dots on the corrugated tiles of the ceiling; I knew, for I had counted them many times. On the walls there was no hospital-supplied artwork, only cards and pictures drawn by my students back at Washington Elementary School in Union City. There was a clock, too, a twelve-inch round face framed with black metal. The thing stared at me. It was one of those institutional clocks with a slow, metallic tick, reminding me of the metronome that ticked away on the Steinway piano.

Here the clock ruled. I would fix my eyes on it, counting how long it would take for the meds to kick in, how long before another shot, a change of bandages, a new shift of nurses, a surgical procedure or visitors. Sometimes, while searching for things to occupy my time, I would press my fingers into my neck to synchronize the blood pulsing with the tick of the clock.

It wasn't long before I was severely depressed, and it came to a head that New Year's Eve of 1975. Don Goldman would come to the hospital and sit with me, read to me, watch television with me. But I could see the expression of pity on his face, could see him turn away from me. Dad likewise would bring in my favorite foods, show me photos, and tell me stories. But I also knew that he was heartbroken to see his "little girl" suffer so.

Over and over, the same thoughts played on my mind. What kind of life would I have, disabled and disfigured? The memory of what I was before the fire and the recognition of what I had become tore me up. Especially hard was seeing old pictures of myself on the wall. The thought of being wheelchair-bound sickened me, as did the thought of returning to the clutches of an overbearing mother. Returning to the house in Teaneck—told what to eat, what to wear, who to date, and how to spend my money? No. I had lost any hope of being my own person. The old Carole was gone forever.

I did have a steady stream of visitors: Mom, Mike, Dad, and Don. But I was causing those I loved so much pain. I knew I looked like a freak. I had wires entering veins in my head, arms, chest. Speared with too many needles, the veins were now collapsing, refusing to be speared one more time. I could see my hip bones, ribs protruding. I imagined myself a relic from a death camp and became convinced there was no life after burns.

That night, after Don and my parents left, I put on the television and watched the revelers. A nurse's aide stayed up with me, talking and reading to me till the wee hours, when I drifted off to sleep. It was a kindness in response to something I had told him—that I would find a way to kill myself.

          *   *   *

"My daughter doesn't want to live," my stricken mother told a surgeon in the burn unit on New Year's Day, 1976.

"Give her reasons to live," was the doctor's terse reply.

This woman despised and dreaded animals. But in her desperation, she hit upon an idea that would save my life. Using a photograph my father had taken, she made a poster—about eight inches by ten inches—and mounted it on my hospital room wall. It contained a picture of my beloved gelding, Bailey. Beneath his photo, she had scrawled in big bold letters, HE WILL CARRY YOU.

Asked later how she came upon this idea, she would admit that it was, and remains, something of a mystery. Unlike my father, my mother never saw Bailey.

"I guess," she later told me, "I was grasping at straws." My mother told me that I would walk, ride, do everything with Bailey.

The poster became an inspiration for me. If my legs wouldn't carry me around, Bailey's would. The one thing I'd be able to do was sit on the back of a horse and ride. Hope was now spelled h-o-r-s-e.

My father also got in on the act. He would go out to the stables, take pictures of Bailey prancing in the snow, and show those photos to me. Under each photo he would write, "Prescription: Take one Bailey daily." Or he'd bring in shots of his boat, and write below, "The *Miss Jene II* is waiting for you." These were "the vessels," he said, that would cart me around once I got out of the hospital. Later, my father would put up a poster on my hospital room wall. "Life gives you lemons," it read, "to make lemonade."

One of the first consequences of fire is weight loss. Within a month, I had lost thirty-two pounds. The body of the burn victim becomes hypermetabolic, the respiratory rate doubles, and the patient—who may have difficulty swallowing a teaspoon of fluid—must somehow consume more than 3,500 calories a day. The body loses protein through all those wounds, yet requires extra calories for healing. Thus the classic burn victim diet is high in both proteins and carbohydrates. The challenge is keeping flesh on bone, never mind fueling the will to live.

The task of feeding became herculean, and it fell mostly to my mother. There would be no designated visiting hours; my family was free to visit between 8:00 A.M. and 10:00 P.M. My father and mother would go to Bischoff's on Cedar Lane in Teaneck and get me a malted shake made with double-yolk farmers' eggs, with ice cream for added protein. I used a straw.

"Draw, draw," my mother would say to me. Or she would use a spoon and hold my tongue. "Swallow, swallow," she would say to me. Back in her kitchen at Teaneck, my mother would broil lamb chops and puree that for me. I loved chicken liver sautéed with onions, with mashed potatoes and gravy, and chicken soup with egg yolks. The hospital even allowed my mother cooking privileges in the nurses' room on that floor, and the smell of her cooking would fill the corridors. She would put the pureed food in my mouth a spoonful at a time. "Chew and swallow," she'd say. "Do it for me."

"No more, I'll vomit," I would sometimes reply.

"Don't vomit," she'd reply.

"Oh, we had a time," my mother recalls.

The calorie requirement loomed each day. It was like running a marathon every day for seven months. The hospital food was, of course, awful. I remember the blue plastic tray, each compartment home to inedible fare. My mother used to call the hospital cafeteria "the garbage disposal," so I was not the only food critic. My mother sought out Jewish delis nearby; my father found a place in Hackensack that made fettucine alfredo, one of my favorite dishes.

I must have balked the first time. "She had one noodle," my father later complained good-naturedly to my mother. "I'll kill that kid." They tried everything—Chinese food, Italian, Jewish. The nurses were often the benefactors of all this largesse. For my birthday in February, my father put on a party for all the nurses and brought in an enormous amount of Chinese food.

"We have an expression in Yiddish," my mother would later explain. "*Oz mir furt schmeert*—If you ride, you have to grease the palm. Daddy was trying to win the nurses over—anything to make life better for you. He was my support. I was your support."

* * *

I would spend more than two hundred days in Hackensack Hospital. In the six months that followed the fire, I faced more surgeries—twenty-eight in all. I also endured the hell of debriding four times a week, and halfway through that schedule, the bath gave way to the sponge. Those were two hundred endless days that tilted between boredom and torture. It was very much like a prison sentence, and I began to long for freedom. When the poster of Bailey went up on my wall, it gave me a focus—something to long for and dream about.

My vantage at that point shifted, shifted miraculously, from inside to outside—from my airless room to hills and fields.

Over and over again, I asked my father to tell of the time he went riding with a friend, reached up to grab a branch as a crop for his buddy, and the horse beneath "left for town," leaving Dad clinging to that branch like some cartoon character. Though the hospital routine, the debriding, the surgeries and medication, all continued as before, I was now yearning for morning light, fresh air, a sunset. I wanted to hear birds singing, I wanted little December licking my face. Above all, I wanted the sweet smell of hay and the grimy smell of my horse.

Eating, and chalking up those 3,500 calories a day, became no easier, but I took to the task with renewed relish. I would put flesh on bone, and damn it all, I would ride my horse.

* * *

Miraculously, the skin grafts were taking. One surgery after another. Waiting for donor sites to regenerate more skin seemed to take forever. Part of the burn team, Dr. Patnaik would make his daily rounds and check—ever so carefully, with his slender fingers—my grafts and donor sites.

Winter had turned to spring as I watched Mom and Dad and Don shed coats for lighter clothing. Covering me with fresh skin had taken half a year, half a year confined to a bed. Would I ever, I thought, be able to move my legs again?

Both the accident and all that time lying in a hospital bed had left my body ill equipped for any kind of motion. Walking was out of the question. Because I had been off my feet for so long, the tendons in my legs had shortened and pulled my heels back, so my feet now pointed down. My left ankle would not move at all, leaving my foot seemingly frozen in place. My toes also locked up and refused to be wiggled. I had no use of my left hand, since I could not touch thumb to forefinger. And after months in hospital I would develop painful pressure sores, or bedsores, which left their mark on me as well. I was a latter-day Job, with all manner of afflictions.

"You were more dead than alive," my mother says. "They had to rebuild you again." And so began the long process of physical therapy that would put me back on my feet.

It started in bed, with weeks of stretching unused tendons into place. Gradually, I was weaned off the catheter and eased into a wheelchair. I would sit at the edge of my bed, and the blood would circulate down my legs, turning them purple and leaving them throbbing as the veins struggled with the flow of blood. I wondered whether my poor feet would bear the little weight I then possessed. Staring at Bailey's poster on the wall, I pondered what strength I would need to groom him, to mount and ride him. In that moment, I made a silent solemn vow to walk out of Hackensack Hospital under my own steam.

The next day I asked the nurses to help me stand. I placed my feet on the floor and tried to put weight on them, but jerked back with the pain.

"You've got to work those legs, get those muscles flexing again," urged Toni Kardell. She well knew how independent I was, and insisted I could do anything I put my mind to. "C'mon, you can do it," Toni would say, "You've got a horse waiting for you to ride."

Tentatively, I placed some pressure on my curled toes and held them there. Gritting my teeth, I stood, then fell and had to be caught by the nurses. This went on for more than an hour, me sobbing, distraught that I could only put weight on my feet for a second or two. Later that afternoon, I again tried to stand. Believe in yourself, I kept repeating in my mind, as if I were chanting a mantra.

One foot down, then the other. Clinging to the nurses, I took a few slow steps and got as far as the sink. It had been a monumental and painful task. Sheer will and determination had got me there. I turned on the faucet and splashed warm water on my face. It was such a simple pleasure, yet it meant so much. I was enjoying the brace of soap and water, reminding myself that my battered body still knew simple joys. It hit me then how accustomed I had grown to being taken care of. Me, who had always prided herself on her independence.

I needed no mirror to tell me how I looked. Petite to begin with, I'd lost enough weight to worry the doctors. Were I a horse, the humane society would have rescued and fed me. My one consolation was knowing that Bailey would not care.

At that moment, Dr. Patnaik came in, saw me standing by the sink, and embraced me. He had been with me from the very beginning of this journey. And I had grown to like him, a soft-spoken man with a gentle touch and an Indian accent. Small and slender—almost frail in his bearing—he would patiently answer all my questions about treatment. And I had many many questions.

I will never forget how overjoyed he was when I took those few steps to the sink, and how unafraid he was to express that joy. Dr. Patnaik immediately called in physical therapists, measured me for crutches, ordered me a walker, and scheduled physical therapy in the PT room downstairs. I was also measured for a Jobst body-suit—medical tights that improve blood circulation and flatten hypertrophic scars by pressing on the skin. Soon I would wear the thing almost around the clock, like a second skin.

That day was a landmark for me. In the evening, Dad celebrated by bringing in a feast of Italian food for Mom, himself, Mike, Don, and me. Dr. Barbara, Dr. Patnaik, and several of my favorite nurses, including Toni, joined us. Dad prodded me to show off by standing again and taking a step or two. To my embarrassment, I obliged. Toni was overcome with emotion; she had been my anchor. And for the first time since I had been admitted to hospital, I saw my mother burst into tears. They were truly tears of joy and relief, tears that were long overdue for her.

Maybe, I thought, with just my father in my corner, I wouldn't have made it. My father was more inclined to be emotional, to break down. My mother would always find something to say, to plant seeds of hope. "We'll find a doctor," she'd say, or "We'll go to the ends of the earth." What unselfishness. She would have died for me.

That day, I told her again that I owed her one. Now was my chance to reassure her. "If it kills me in therapy," I promised her, "I don't care how much it hurts. I'm walking out of here!"

In the weeks to follow, I would learn to walk all over again. Balance was a problem. With my tendons so contracted, I could not place my left foot flat on the floor and instead had to walk on the side of it. And since the grafted skin on my feet was so impossibly tender, I couldn't wear enclosed shoes that would rub on my heels, only sandals.

The tingling, burning sensation continued, making every step painful. Over and over, staff would say, "Here we never say, 'I can't.'" I would hold on to the rails in the PT room, often glancing over at the paraplegics around me. You've got legs, I kept telling myself; you just need to make them work again. And always, there was the thought of Bailey. He would make my legs work again; that much was certain.

*　　*　　*

There were still dark days, but we did find things to laugh about. The flying bed, for instance.

Moving me—to change dressings, to use the bedpan, to reduce the risk of bedsores—was hellish, and so they brought in a special bed from a burn center in New York. The rotating bed had a round steel frame and, like a Ferris wheel, could rotate 360 degrees. Its purpose was to keep the patient's body turned to avoid bedsores. Since the backs of my legs and my buttocks had been burned and skin grafted, I would be turned on my stomach for long periods—and I do mean *lonnnng* periods—to let those parts of my body heal. Sometimes a kind aide would come in and read to me to alleviate the boredom. Though I felt like a piece of chicken on a rotisserie, the rotating bed was doing its job.

Until one day, when my mother got a call from the hospital. "We have a problem with your daughter," my mother recalls someone saying on the other end of the line. Every other day my mother would get calls like this one: "We have a problem with your daughter."

My mother remembers arriving at the hospital that day. There I was, up by the ceiling in this bed, and they couldn't get me down. Not one person in the hospital knew how to work that bed. Finally, someone came from one of the burn centers and pushed whatever buttons were necessary to lower the bed. I had been up there for hours, frightened and lying on my stomach.

Then there was the time the Catholic priest paid a visit. There was a knock on my door, and a man in a collar walked in and said he was there to administer the last rites.

"Not to me, you're not," I told him. "I'm a little Jewish girl. You've got the wrong room. I'm not ready for the last rites." The priest sheepishly backed out, and his mistake became a standing joke for the whole hospital. It was almost as funny as the faith healers whose daughter was also a burn victim and who had targeted my mother for conversion. All the relatives of burn patients would gather in the hospital solarium to tell one another their stories, to console one another, and even to proselytize. "One big unhappy family," my mother called it.

Another time, when my catheter had finally been removed and I was able to use a bedpan on my own, an orderly would routinely come around with juices and sodas—including one I always asked for called "Howdy." A nurse hadn't drawn the curtain around my bed, and I was up on the bed, using the bedpan, my long hospital gown affording me only a little privacy, when the orderly with the drink cart chanced along.

"Howdy?" he asked.

"Doody," I replied.

My father, meanwhile, would play practical jokes on the nurses. He'd put stuffed animals beneath my pillow and stick toilet paper onto chairs with tape, so it would adhere to nurses' derrieres. Somehow, through all this, though not at all in the beginning, he found joy.

There was a pattern to even these darkest of times. Just when the tunnel seemed impossibly long and dark, a light would appear at the end.

There was the time, for example, my mother's beautician came to the hospital. My mother had asked if Vincent, who had cut her own hair for years, would come and cut mine.

"He knew you were a burn victim," my mother began. " 'It'll be a privilege,' he said, 'to cut your daughter's hair.' He came in like a doctor, with a black valise. He put down the case and gowned up in disposable paper clothes, slippers, and mask, as we all had to do before going into your room, and he started to comb your hair.

Long blond hair you had. And when he was through, you had no hair." The surgeries, the anesthesia, had combined to weaken the hair, and the mere touch of the comb uprooted it.

Insult had followed injury.

"You were hysterical," my mother remembers. " 'Now I have no hair,' you cried. 'I don't want to live.' But Vincent was very calm. He said, 'I've known people who've lost every hair on their head. When the hair grows back, it comes back stronger and healthier. You see all this peach fuzz? This is new hair coming in.' He used a mirror to show you. 'You'll have healthier and more beautiful hair than before,' he said. 'Put on a scarf, and you'll look gorgeous.' " My hair, of course, did come back, and, as Vincent had predicted, stronger and healthier.

I was reminded often during those impossibly long days and months in Hackensack Hospital of that adage, "What doesn't kill you makes you stronger."

*　　　*　　　*

Early in June, during the seventh month of my captivity at Hackensack Hospital, I was given a walker to use, and I soon prided myself on using the toilet on my own, on brushing my teeth, on bathing. They seemed such earthly pleasures. I practiced walking down the hallway of the fourth floor, the floor I had been on for so many months, which I now set out to explore. The solarium, where my family had spent so much time waiting and worrying (and ducking the entreaties of faith healers), the nurses' room where my mother had cooked for me, the long corridors: the world beyond my sterile domain was finally opening up to me.

On June 11, 1976, some 4,824 hours after being wheeled into Hackensack Hospital in an ambulance, I emerged, stabbing the ground with my walker. Family and hospital staff had gathered to cheer me on, clapping and praising me for being so courageous and such a "model patient" (apparently I had been forgiven for being an "incorrigible" one). I felt for the first time in almost seven months the sun on my face, felt the light wind, smelled the air, the flowers, the fresh-cut grass—treasures, every one.

I was outside. And I was going home.

6

Bailey to the Rescue

HOME AS I KNEW IT before the fire had vanished. Gone were my independence (and the car and job that enabled it), and the privacy and freedom I had enjoyed for four years in that old rental house in River Edge. Going back to the ranch house in Teaneck was like going back to my childhood, to being totally dependent on my parents. And though I was happy to be free of the hospital, great sadness and resignation marked my return to that pink room in Teaneck.

My mother still ruled this roost (and its "rooster," my father) and the No Pets rule still applied. The Bailey poster had been a stroke of genius, but my mother had not changed her personal view that pets in her home posed a dire threat to prized carpets and sofas. Despite my protests, and my father's offer to feed and walk her, my dog, December, was not allowed to come home with me. She would have to stay where she was—at the home of Don's parents.

It was mortifying to be in that old homestead at the age of

twenty-nine. My mother would bathe and dress me, then dash off to her store (she was in the midst of selling the business). My father would chauffeur me to my triweekly physical therapy sessions and to my psychological counselor, Dr. Tom Craig. I had forgotten—until I hobbled into the foyer of our house—how many mirrors there were—in the entryway, the dining room, the bedrooms. Wherever I went, I faced my own image. I was disabled and disfigured, and the combination was crippling in every way.

Don Goldman would drop by several times a week to keep me company. I was appreciative of his caring and friendship, grateful for the attention of a male—especially one who had saved my life. But Don was a lost soul. He had graduated several years beforehand from the University of Miami—rumored to be the ultimate party school—and, after bouncing from job to job, was back living at home. He lacked ambition, my mother complained. He hadn't found himself yet, his parents explained.

For all kinds of reasons, our relationship would not last the summer. What a coat of guilt he must have worn, flogging himself for an accident he believed he should have prevented. I never held him accountable; on the contrary, I knew he had saved my life. Whatever pain he felt, and whatever the cause, he assuaged it as best he could with recreational drugs. I, too, had pain. I was, or so the mirrors told me, a regular circus sideshow, with crew-cut hair, pulled-down lip, and rattlesnake skin, hobbling about on crutches, my fingers bent and stiff like wet leather gloves left too long on a frozen pond.

One day, Don came to the house in Teaneck.

"I have a surprise for you," he said.

He took me to his parents' house, where his mother greeted me with a single red rose and refused my offer of money for dog food. December—I had not seen her in more than eight months—ran to greet me, whining excitedly, running around me in circles, and licking my face when Don brought her closer.

Then he guided me over to the garage, raised the door, and unveiled his surprise. There it was. The '53 Porsche Super Coupe, resurrected and reassembled, all white and gleaming. I was speechless, overcome with mixed emotions.

"Happy to see the old girl?" he asked, smiling wide. "Nick and I got it running, good as new!"

My words came out in slow bursts. "I'm . . . not sure . . . I ever want to . . . drive it again. I don't . . . even know if I can."

"Sure you can," he came back. "When I first met you, you had that Yamaha motorcycle you used to cruise around on, remember? You're the only girl I know who can ride just about anything. Didn't you always say your life motto was 'Whenever you get thrown, get back on!' Nothing stops the Carole I know."

I like to think now he was right. Though the Porsche was freighted with symbolism—the machine had almost cost me my life—I did keep it for several years. It seems I wanted to cling to some shred of what I had before the accident.

After lunch that day, I gave December a bath, and we all sat outside for a while, throwing a tennis ball for her to fetch. I was wearing my Jobst bodysuit that day, as I would twenty-three hours a day for the next two years, only removing it to bathe myself or clean the suit. I had even dared to wear the Jobst face mask because I was told it would reduce my facial scarring. But in it I felt inhuman, transformed into an alien or a thief who wears panty hose over his face. My face was my passport, my identity. And judging from people's reactions to that face, I wanted to crawl in a hole and hide.

That day, when the pressure garment grew too hot under the summer sun, Don drove me back to my parents' home in the Porsche and left the car there. The white beauty sat in the driveway, impressive in the afternoon light. Only later did I notice the key chain, which featured a baby bird ready to fly the nest. The caption beneath the photo read, "He can because he thinks he can."

※　　　※　　　※

I had only been home a few weeks when my mother dropped a bombshell. Aunt Rose, Uncle Herbie, Aunt Pearl, and my cousin Susan were all coming over for a visit and a meal. I had been too long in the company of people used to my appearance, and the thought of an extended family visit filled me with dread.

"Carole," my mother argued, "these are your family, those who love you. They're only happy to see you alive. They've been waiting a long time to see you."

I donned my wig and best gray sweatpants for the Sunday brunch. We sat in the living room, and I was grateful for the constant babble and the chance to be filled in on family news. But their averted looks spoke of their fright at seeing my red, raw, and angry scars. I took every whisper as a comment on the way I looked. One entire wall of the living room was mirrored, so I strategically took a seat where I didn't have to face myself. There was the usual meal of assorted bagels, cream cheese, lox, and other smoked fish, but I barely touched mine, fearful that with my scarred lip, food or drink would spill out. It was a bad scene, as we used to say in those days, and it was about to get worse.

Without warning, my mother asked, "Carole, how about playing something for us on the piano?"

My father darted her a look. "Jene," he said, frowning and shaking his head.

I shrank. How could she do this to me? I thought. Make a spectacle of me in my hideous condition. The dark mahogany Steinway baby grand, an old friend, loomed large in one corner of the living room, untouched since the last time I had played—more than a year beforehand.

"That's all right, Dad!" I said, wincing as I eased myself up slowly and got to my feet. Mike handed me the crutches, and I made my way slowly to the piano. I opened up the cover, exposing the keys, ran my right hand over them and played a scale. The piano was badly out of tune, but I eked out the melody of Claude Debussy's "The Children's Corner" for a minute or two. But my left hand was absolutely useless, the fingers contracted and bent like a bear's paw. I shut the cover down. "Sorry," I said, "it's out of tune."

In the silence that followed, I caught my father's sidelong glance, his eyes filling with tears.

My mother's anger flared. "Irv, you've got to stop this crying," she said and looked away from him.

"What?" he asked.

"Stop feeling sorry for her. Pity won't help her at all."

"You're unbelievable, Jene," he said, then helped me up. I excused myself and went to my room. And so ended, disastrously, my first public appearance in the wake of the fire. I could hear my relations saying their good-byes, talking about me in the foyer. Was I in pain? Taking medication? Did I need more surgeries? Could they help in any way? So this, I thought, is how it would be from now on. People would always be afraid to ask these things up front. I'd be a thing to pity. How did that Linda Rondstadt song go? "Poor poor pitiful me."

The next morning, after a physical therapy session at the hospital, my father suggested we stop in at Holly's—our old haunt—for their special, fried chicken in a basket. I shrugged. But my indifference turned to panic when we got inside and I saw the crowd. My father would later tell me he felt the same surge of fear, and he regretted not calling ahead to warn the owners—the Soloways—not to ask any embarrassing questions.

A middle-aged man with his wife and two young children looked at my crutches and offered me his seat, which I declined, though he insisted. I blushed at this, all the while thinking that the only positive thing about my red facial scars was that no one could tell I was blushing. I remembered what Mark Twain had written: "Man is the only animal that blushes. Or needs to."

Soon the polite man's owl-eyed kids started gawking at me, talking in small whispers. Their open stares were more painful than my skin grafts. "What happened to you?" the younger one asked, overcome by curiosity.

"I'm so sorry," whispered her mother, pulling her daughter away.

"It's okay," I said, though my smile could not hide my humiliation.

Then the girl's sister launched her own inquiry. "What's wrong with that girl?"

A few minutes later, Mr. Soloway breezed by and sat with us at our usual green leather booth, the one with the view of the giant neon chicken running into a basket. He, at least, got it right. Mr. Soloway asked how I was doing and seemed his normal cheerful self. I had my usual: the fried chicken basket and french fries, and, for dessert, a sundae topped with Holly's pink-and-green whipped cream.

My eyes drifted over the other green Formica tables, hoping against hope that I would not see people I knew. I kept my eyes downcast for the rest of the meal, intent on sparing any friends, and myself, the embarrassment of an encounter. Friends of my father stopped by to chat, but they were clearly uncomfortable. They looked out the window, at other tables—anything but at the one thing they wanted to look at. Even my father seemed rattled by the long silences between us. We had always talked so freely.

I remembered what Dr. Craig, the counselor at the hospital, had said. "Tell them it's okay to look," he had advised me. "It's okay to ask you questions."

But it wasn't okay. I didn't want people to look at me or to ask questions. I never had been one to draw attention to myself. If I wanted people to look at me, it would be because I possessed uncommon beauty or talent. I had lost both. What I wanted was a mask—that and a new hand and foot.

That night I wrote a poem in my journal. I called it "Eyes," and it read, in part,

All eyes are on me.
Strange eyes,
sympathetic eyes . . .
eyes of buttons on blouses,
eyes of faces on watches,
eyes of holes in shoes . . .
Is there no escape
from these eyes?

Another poem, written on August 3, 1976, and called "Mask," imagines me at a costume ball and has everyone at the appointed hour removing his or her mask—except me. "And I remain / all alone / unable to remove my mask of scars."

"Different," written at about the same time, captures my state of mind. It begins,

I am a rough almond
among exquisite hickories.
a venus fly-trap
among daisies,
an isolated spade
in a hand of hearts,
a circle among squares . . .
I am different,
I am scarred.

Why hadn't I seen a burned or severely disfigured person in public before? Now I understood why. They hide. Nothing I had been through in hospital prepared me for my entrance into the community. Some stared, especially when I wore the Jobst face mask. Others quickly looked away or gasped in horror. They saw the disfigurement, not me.

"I've been thinking about Bailey," I said over dinner the night following the calamitous family gathering. "I want to see him."

There was a pause.

"Carole," my mother began, "maybe when you're a little stronger. It doesn't have to be—"

"I want to go see him tomorrow," I interjected. "It's been ages. He's probably forgotten me by now. Please, Dad. Take me to the stable tomorrow?"

My request had a pleading note, but there was also determination in my voice. My mother got up from the table and cleared the dishes. My father nodded his assent. That night I held Bailey's picture in my hand and thought of him as I fell into a deep sleep.

The next morning a soft, warm rain fell as we drove the blue Buick station wagon to Mar-Bel's Stable, twenty minutes from home. Mud splattered the car's wheel wells as we turned up the drive. In several of the paddocks horses bobbed their heads, counting down the time to lunch. The rain and mud seemed to have dissuaded riders from their morning workouts. A black dog lifted his head to see who had arrived, but he must have sensed we weren't intruders. He set his head back down on his paws and continued to ponder the leaves and insect life.

*   *   *

With Dad's help, I swung my legs out the door, and then my crutches. I started for the barn, eyes locked on the dirt ahead, surveying the surface for traps. Only the Tingleys—the brand name of the rubber overshoes I had put on over my sandals—spared my sweatpants from the mud.

A dozen steps beyond the car, I paused in my labor and stood still for a moment, lifting my face to the warm air and the familiar aroma and sweet smell of timothy-alfalfa hay. As I listened to a tattletale bluejay competing with the sound of the rain, an orange marmalade cat came over and rubbed himself on my leg.

In the first stall, a liver chestnut shifted his weight from one back hoof to another, his muzzle grazing the top rail of his stall. I made my way past him and down the shed-row aisle to where I knew my golden horse was likely snoozing. In black marking pen, long before the accident, I had put a sign on his stall, "Half Grain Ration Only at Night." Bailey did tend to fat. On seeing me come toward him, he put his head out of the stall and nickered softly, deep in his throat, his lower lip trembling in anticipation of the carrot he spotted in my hand. Without saying a word, I slipped him some carrot and stroked his forehead, cradling his head like a found treasure. I wrapped my arms around his neck, pressed my face into his satin coat, and took long breaths. I wanted to inhale him. From my hospital bed and for a very long time, I had tried to imagine this moment; now it had arrived. A solitary tear ran down my face.

"You haven't forgotten me at all, have you, Bailey?" I asked him. I looked around and took in the fresh shavings and full bucket of water. I looked at my horse's muscular flanks, glistening like wet silk. There was plenty of flesh over his ribs, no sign of protruding bones. Horsemen have a saying, "The best color on a horse is fat." It was obvious he was being well cared for.

Just then a door opened, and in walked Melly (short for Melvin) Pinera, the stable owner. An ex-boxer with steel gray hair and a weathered mug, he was younger in heart than half the men his age I knew, and kinder than all of them put together. Though taciturn with strangers, he was affable with people he knew. And I liked his priorities. Melly ran an organized barn. He was good to his animals and put them above showy displays. There were no brass stall plates here, no monogrammed hats and jackets for stable hands to wear, no matching halters.

"We've all been waiting for this day, Carole," he said. "Especially Bailey." Melly knew to expect us, for Dad had called ahead.

"You've taken great care of him," I said. "He looks wonderful. I can see he's getting his share of that fifty-pound bag of carrots over there." Melly took better care of his horses than most parents took care of their children. He was the kind of man who made sure his horses had their meals before he had his. Melly had taken in many rescue horses—horses that had been abused or mistreated, allowed to waste away in fields—and brought them back to physical and psychological good health. He was, in every way, a proud horse-man.

Bailey, meanwhile, rolled in his clean shavings for about ten seconds, then groaned and struggled to his feet, leaving confetti-like pieces in his long mane and tail. He was aging but still good-looking. The long shadow of time had been kind to him.

"Trouble is," said Melly, "he's getting fat and lazy. Too bad he's so fast." Melly shot a glance at Dad and winked. Bailey cocked a rear leg, half closed his eyes, and settled into a doze.

"Fast asleep, you mean," countered my father. He reached over to stroke the gelding's neck. Bailey surfaced from sleep long enough to come at a fly on his barrel, both swishing his tail around and turning his head to bite the offending bug.

"Mind if I go in the stall with him, Melly?" I asked. It seemed strange to be asking someone else's permission to visit with my own horse, but it had been so long. With my permission, Melly had been using Bailey for lessons. I had the sense that Bailey's ownership had shifted from me just a little. Physically, I also felt some uncertainty. More than anything, I was looking for Melly's blessing.

"Not at all," he replied. "I'll get you a chair so you can sit a spell with him." Melly walked down the aisle and came back with a tall stool. I undid the door latch, and Dad opened the stall door before placing the stool just inside. He stayed right there, just in case Bailey took a notion to go for a stroll. I propped myself up on the stool and handed the crutches to my father.

Unlike many horses who become wide-eyed or worse at the sight of strange things in their stalls, Bailey was unfazed by any of this. A lesson horse for six years before I got him, he was as close to bombproof as a horse could get. Horse people call such horses "packers," and the word is used admiringly.

"This is your lucky day, Bailey," I said, scratching his neck. He nickered with pleasure. I knew this horse well—his pleasures, his pains, his wants and desires, the little wildness and mischief that sometimes came over him. I had found the spot that he really enjoyed having rubbed; most horses have one, and sometimes several. Bailey would let me know I was on the money by stretching his lips far out and softly clacking together his upper and lower teeth. This was horse language for "Aaaahhhhhhhhhhhhhh."

Then came his lunch of carrots. I knew the seductive power a carrot had on a horse. I believed in treating a horse with kindness, but I also believed in making him mind his manners. I had, for example, taught Bailey to take carrots from my hand gently. He munched on a couple of big ones, dribbling carrot crumbs out the side of his mouth.

"I see we have a lot in common," I joked, earning a smile from Dad, who then started chatting with Melly. My finger started tracing the single whorl on Bailey's forehead, just between and above his eyes. The noted trainer Linda Tellington-Jones has a theory that the pattern of whorls on a horse's face can reveal his personality. Bailey's whorls spoke of his uncomplicated and trustworthy nature.

I stayed there with Bailey, and without any bidding he laid his massive head in my lap and used it for a pillow. That was his way of caressing me. In that moment I knew where my sanctuary lay.

*   *   *

A few nights later I asked my father if he'd take me to the stable to see Bailey again. This time I was going to ride. Again, my mother objected, and on the same grounds as last time: "Shouldn't you wait until you're stronger?"

"Closed subject," was my reply, and I raised my hand to end discussion. My father grinned in approval.

We got there early the next day, before the summer sun could get to work on my face and hands, which were already lobster red. I also hoped to avoid other riders, since my getup was hardly high equestrian fashion. I wore a baseball cap, a long-sleeved button-down shirt, and sweatpants tucked into Tingleys over sandals and tied with shoelaces. As we arrived, a stable hand had just finished mucking out the last stall and was starting to turn out horses into their paddocks. The sky that day was a chambray blue, shot through with faint gray clouds. A perfect day to ride.

Bailey was in his stall, vacuuming up the last bit of hay from breakfast. When he saw me, he came to the stall door and nickered. He was a vocal horse, one who loved being with people. I had been drawn to him for that very reason; that, and his easy manner.

"How ya doin', fella?" I asked him, peering into his eyes. I had been around horses long enough to know that mindless chatter is as soothing to horses as a caress.

I turned on my crutches and headed for the tack room, where I breathed in the heady and welcome scent of leather emanating from all the saddles and bridles. Beyond the shining array of bits, old Courbettes, and a gloriously tooled Mexican saddle with an acorn design, was my own. The flawless basket-weave Tex Tan looked as new as it had the day I bought it, with the bridle and matching breast collar lying over the horn.

A shiver went up my spine when I saw that saddle. I ran my fingertips over the seat. Melly had kept it cleaned and oiled—as if it were his own, my father told me. The weight of the leather-covered stirrups felt promising, for I knew my feet would be strengthened in their embrace. I smiled, wishing Melly were here so I could thank him.

Dad did what I still couldn't do. He went into Bailey's stall, put
a halter and lead rope on him, led him over to the cross-ties, and
snapped them onto the side brass rings of the halter. (Anchored in
the aisle's wooden supports, cross-ties are lengths of light chain
attached to the horse's halter to allow grooming or work by the farrier.) I set my crutches against a wall, grabbed a brush, and hobbled
over to my horse's left shoulder. I put all my weight on my right
foot—the one I could set down flat—and kept my left hand on Bailey for balance. I was making this up as I went, but my method
seemed to work. It felt good to brush Bailey all over, starting, as
always, at the neck and working my way back to the tail. Then I did
the other side. When he was clean to my satisfaction, I brushed his
long white mane, which all fell flat on that side.

"Did you ever hear," my father asked me, "that a horse is more
supple on the side his mane naturally falls on?"

"No. Is that really true?"

"Well," he explained, "I've heard that even racehorses prefer to
take their leads on their mane side. Who knows? Maybe it's an old
trainer's tale."

There was a ritual order to tacking up a horse. First brush, then
pick out the feet, then saddle up. As I started to clean Bailey's
unshod hooves, I could feel the strain on my back muscles. By the
fourth foot, I was lathered in sweat. Next came the saddle pad,
which I settled gently on Bailey's back so the front part just covered
his withers. Dad then dropped the saddle gingerly onto the pad. I
joked to my father that my newly grafted skin (known as "mesh
grafts") was a good match for the saddle's basket-weave design. It
took a little creativity to cinch up the saddle: I used one finger of

my left hand to hold the ring while my right hand made the required knot in the leather. The bridle was easy. Bailey, good-mannered horse that he was, lowered his head and accepted the snaffle bit.

At the mounting block inside the ring, he stood patiently while Dad held the reins. I used the stool as a walker to get me to the mounting block, but here I paused as I leaned on the saddle horn for balance. My throat closed up, my shoulders squared up around my neck. It's a test of courage to get on the back of a thousand-pound animal while you're feeling frail. Riding horses, you come to know that there are many such times, when desire overcomes fear. Drawing a deep breath, I put my left foot in the wide stirrup, leaned my torso forward, and cautiously swung my right leg in an arc over the saddle. I eased my body down like a robin landing on its nest. And there I sat, motionless. Bailey hadn't moved an inch. I breathed a sigh of relief, locked my right hand around the reins, and told Dad to let go.

It's like that moment when you're a child and the training wheels have just that day come off the bike. Cockiness has got you to this point, but cockiness alone will not banish fear. The moment my father let go of the reins, I was on my own.

I nudged Bailey with my heels, and he cocked his ears back at me. In equine terms, he was saying, "Now what?" No doubt he hadn't felt my weak legs urging him forward. Teeth clenched, I tried again. Still no response.

"He's lazy enough to have slept through Pearl Harbor," my father teased. He handed me a crop, and Bailey perked up notice-ably. I tapped him by my right leg, pressed my heels into his barrel, and made a kissing sound to send him forward. We walked slowly around the rail that defined the ring, my eyes fixed straight ahead. He had done this so often, like an an old milk horse with a twenty-year route fixed in his brain. But that day he put a smile on my face. I had shifted just a little: a cautious and downtrodden woman was at least moving in the direction of bold and assured rider.

Bailey seemed to sense that he had someone needy on his back. I knew he would never hurt anyone through malice; the remarkable compassion he had shown me was evident in his gentleness. My father stood back and watched, a tear on his cheek, the emotion of the moment washing over him. From a distance I heard clapping, slow and loud. I turned in that direction and spotted Melly, who was also clearly moved by the moment. In that low, raspy voice of his, he said, "Looks like you've found the best therapist of all!"

"The best medicine in the world," I replied. "That's my sermon on the mount!" We all laughed at my pun.

I remember when I first got out of the hospital, someone had given me a book written by a rabbi, *When Bad Things Happen to Good People*. I wasn't really interested in the *why* of it all; the shedding of tears offered no relief, and anger got me nowhere. Some days I struggled to get out of bed, and I fell into despair.

This much I knew: I needed to stop thinking about myself, my pain, my fears. I needed to distill a blessing out of all this pain. And what I would discover, slowly and gradually, in the years to come, is that when I spent time with my horse, I was no longer a burn victim.

On the back of a horse I was strong and graceful. Bailey was carrying me far away from my sense of hopelessness. On his back, I felt no pain. On his back, I was well again. I knew I would become stronger in my legs and in my posture. More importantly, I would regain my passion for life, my joy. There was a chance to be part of the real world again. It amazed me then, and still does, that this largest of domesticated animals would allow me—a waiflike, frail rider—to guide him with a mere touch of the reins and legs.

On the back of a horse I was a horsewoman and, later, a horse trainer. Anger would eventually give way to the calming sight of horses grazing in a pasture, and despair would succumb to the promise of an early-morning ride. As for self-obsession, I was far too busy trying to fathom the mind of the horse I was riding. The horse would become my healer.

7

Horses Don't Stare

THE SUMMER OF 1976 and the several years that followed were much about *d*-words: *disabled, disfigured, depressed.* A few *h* words would loom large as well: *hospital, healing, horses.* Curiously, a single smell had the power to conjure both hospital and horse: Betadine, an alcohol-based disinfectant used as a presurgical scrub but also painted on the underside of horses' hooves against fungal infections. I would catch a whiff of Betadine in the stable and, though surrounded by horses and the sweet smell of hay, be drawn right back to Hackensack Hospital.

My body was a prison then. My face, left hand, and left foot would all require major—and many—reconstructive surgeries, and until they were dealt with, I was the object of stares. Bailey offered relief from such unwanted attention. My horse meant that I could shift focus, away from me and all my troubles. Bailey was a living, breathing creature I could enjoy and relate to. He was a friend and companion who accepted me. Above all, he did not stare.

My horse provided me with something people could not. Even my own mother, as supportive as she was, became acutely aware of people staring at me. "Put long sleeves on," she would say. Horses, on the other hand, didn't care about scar tissue or useless hands and feet. My horse accepted me as I was.

Whenever I had to talk or cry, I went to see Bailey. I would go into his stall, drag that troublesome foot of mine (like a ball on the end of a chain), and lead him toward the barn aisle cross-ties at Mar-Bel. I took comfort in his apple breath and kind eyes. And while grooming his lustrous coat, I would look deep into Bailey's eyes and tell him my problems. There wasn't anything about me that Bailey didn't hear about. And he kept my secrets oh, so well. I'd tell him of my fears—fear of impending surgeries and of more pain, fears of rejection by men. And I would put to him the questions that still plagued me. Why did this accident happen to me? Was I supposed to learn something from it? And if so, what?

The physical pain I had felt, if nothing else, was honest and open. But there were other kinds of pain, too. A few weeks after I left the hospital, my friend Jan had called and seemed anxious to see me. Bearing a small nosegay of flowers, she looked perky and trim in her faded Levi's and T-shirt. Jan spoke animatedly, and then her face turned from red to ghost-white, and her eyes welled with tears.

"Carole," she said, "I have something to tell you. I'm so ashamed of myself. I slept with your boyfriend. I slept with Don while you were in the hospital."

It was as if she had thrown a glass of ice-cold water in my face. When I finally gathered myself to ask her why, she said something about trying to comfort each other in the wake of my accident. Jan couldn't bear the guilt and hoped for forgiveness, but I had none to offer. When she closed the door of our house in Teaneck, I knew it was the last time I would ever see her.

※   ※   ※

Later, I would cry into my horse's thick white mane and hang on his neck. Bailey just listened. He did not counter with arguments or advice. Nickering softly, he let me know I was loved and needed. He was my closest and most trusted companion, my spiritual adviser—mute but eloquent. At this point in my life I thought that Bailey and December were the only beings capable of understanding me.

It occurred to me that Bailey was a projection of my own dreams. He was everything I was not: strong, powerful, beautiful. He had the unique ability to allow me to escape from my mundane—and so acutely *medical*—existence. Some days we would ride for a long time. When Bailey and I loped across the open fields, we were one body, one heart, racing against the wind. Best was around sunset, when I felt bathed in peace, sharing this glorious moment with my horse. Sitting on his back, I could touch the sky—even if I couldn't walk. On Bailey's back, I felt a little closer to the divine.

※   ※   ※

Wanted: Good surgeon(s) to put Humpty Dumpty back together again. That might have been the wording of my classified ad as summer came to a close in 1976, and I started making my rounds of plastic and reconstructive surgeons. My face and foot could be rebuilt later; what I needed first was to regain use of that left hand so I could fasten buttons, dress myself, and win back some of the precious independence I had lost.

First stop was a famous surgeon on Fifth Avenue who had been highly recommended by Dr. Barbara. In that chic uptown office, decorated smartly in pink and black, amid the abstract art and shiny chrome furniture, I sat with my mother and leafed through an album of before-and-after photographs of patients posed beside this Dr. Kildare lookalike. Also in the album were magazine articles describing his celebrity patients and their rhinoplasties, liposuctions, tummy tucks, face-lifts, and a host of other cosmetic jobs. But the dapper doctor had no experience with burn victims. Even before my cursory visit, I knew he wasn't for me.

Then I tried a "plastic surgeon to the stars" in Miami, not far from my parents' condominium in Fort Lauderdale. This doctor was older than the other one, and I tagged him in my mind as Marcus Welby, M.D. This time my father accompanied me, but the story was the same. Same magazines and photo albums, different celebrities. A few port-wine-stain jobs, a couple of cleft-palate repairs. Any burn victims? Not one.

Finally, a fellow teacher in Teaneck told me about a former classmate of her husband's, a hand specialist in training at Massachusetts General Hospital. Of course. Why had we not thought of this hospital, which was so closely affiliated with the Shriners' Burn Center? My mother, father, and I drove up to Boston as soon as we could book an appointment with Dr. Benjamin Cohen in Mass General's Department of Plastic and Reconstructive Surgery.

I remember being overwhelmed by the size of the hospital. If Hackensack was a village, Mass General was a veritable city. Waiting to meet me was a team of surgeons, including Dr. John Constable, head of plastic and reconstructive surgery, and Dr. Cohen, a reconstructive hand specialist. Having struck out with doctors Kildare and Welby, I made it my first order of business to inquire about their collective experience with burn victims. The expressions on their faces said everything. I was embarrassed even to have asked. Nevertheless, I did pore over an album of photographs showing their reconstructive work on burn patients. The team then examined me from head to toe, discussing among themselves all that had to be done to my face, hand, and foot. Dr. Constable, a tall and refined Englishman, told me that while there was severe tendon damage to my hand, he thought it was possible to regain partial use.

The hand, he explained, is one of the most difficult parts of the body to operate on—precisely because the hand is so versatile. I kept looking at his own hand, with its long, slim fingers, for these were the hands that would operate on my poor paw. I liked everything about Dr. Constable: his experience (he was in his late fifties), his manner (warm and reassuring), his collegiality (he stressed that he was part of a team of doctors, with him as its head). Above all, I admired his honesty. He wanted no false hope. He was optimistic about the outcome for my face, less so about the hand. I might gain some function in my left hand, he said, but it would never return to its former state. And while he expressed amazement that I'd made it through seven months of skin grafting, he also warned me that the real job of rebuilding my body was about to begin.

How right he was: four years later, I was still going under the knife.

   ❁   ✿   ❁

As for Dr. Cohen, he was a bright young intern with a short, blocky build, dark hair, and a wide smile. I connected with him, for it seemed I could make him laugh. Once, while he and others were musing aloud on where to harvest skin for my chin and hand, I suggested that surely they could leave my poor skin be and instead gather up all the foreskins left over from circumcisions at the hospital and use *them* for the next graft! I told the doctors I would write a story of my adventure, that it would be called "Dr. Foreskinstein" and would one day be made into a movie starring Gene Wilder. I later wrote the story and gave a copy to Dr. Cohen. (He must have appreciated my bizarre sense of humor, for we happened to meet years later in Houston, Texas—where he had set up practice—and he seemed overjoyed to see me. He introduced me to all his partners and showed me off as if I were a former, and well-remembered, pupil.)

I had good people in my corner. For the first time in many months, I felt a sense of hope. Not just relief that I had finally found the right team of doctors, but the possibility that these gifted and compassionate physicians could actually recast me. These doctors had already accomplished their first miracle: they had planted a smile on my face.

My sessions with Bailey—three a week—were also producing smiles. On days I felt too weak to ride, I groomed him, giving my arms a good workout. Once Melly walked by as I was deploying the curry brush (used in a circular motion to raise dirt and produce a shine on the horse's coat). "Any shinier," he said, "and we'll all have to wear sunglasses to look at your horse." I was discovering an old truth: a good horse will banish melancholy.

With Bailey as companion, I was enjoying the sweet and exhilarating effects of fresh air and exercise. My troubles were temporarily out of mind. I was still frail, but I was steadily gaining strength in my legs and arms, and my horse was providing me with a newfound sense of power. I would need all of it in the days ahead.

I was also facing fear every time I rode my horse. Experience and age had calmed Bailey, but with horses there are no guarantees. They get frightened, they startle, they bolt, rear, and buck. Horses are animals of prey, and they possess a flight instinct. Riding, then, can be dangerous, very dangerous. Even the calmest horse can spook and spin, or move right out from under you at the sight of deer leaping nearby or wild turkeys flying up in front of him.

Ask any horseman how his horse reacts when "the furniture is rearranged." Let's say that the horse passes the same things in the arena every day, and then one day a new manure spreader appears. Some horses eye it, others stop dead in their tracks, others—especially young horses—will shy or jump way from it. Bailey was a relatively calm horse, but he could still react to things around him, and I had to be ready for anything to happen. I had to be on guard all the time, alert and intuitive, quickly reacting to the horse. Confronting my fears with a horse helped me to confront the other fears in my life—about surgeries and outcomes.

There were still periods of darkness, but now there was some light, too. I have two photographs from that time, both from the same roll of film, for the color is distinctive. A reddish hue marks all the images. One was a strange shot, taken in a kitchen, of chicken pieces with a butcher knife alongside. I took this photograph, and it's quite revealing of my mindset in those days. After all those surgeries, my mind likely addled from all the morphine, I felt like a piece of meat.

Another image has me back in the hospital, this time hamming it up. I'm about to undergo reconstructive surgery, and I'm thinking, If they're going to rebuild my face, how about my breasts too? I have inserted two pointy objects beneath my hospital gown (imagine roadside construction pylons planted at my chest). For many years during this stretch, there was little to laugh at. What laughter there was, was precious.

And it came from unexpected sources—a parrot, for instance. During this time, I went with my father and visited Parrot Jungle in Miami. Fascinated by the colorful birds, I watched as a young man put on a show to illustrate their intelligence and clever mimicry. Birds played dead, roller-skated, did impersonations. Later, I approached one of the birds as he sat on top of his cage, nibbling a peanut in its shell. The parrot, whose name was Bobo, looked at me and said, "Pretty girl!" Looking around to see if there were other females present, I replied, "Are you nuts?"

To which he responded, "Bobo likes nuts!"

＊　　＊　　＊

By the time my mother and I returned to Boston for the first surgery, the leaves had turned their brilliant reds and yellows and golds. I would need a light jacket, but I was unable to get my left hand through the sleeve of any coat we tried. The frozen claw would not budge; eventually we found a cape that would go over my head and did the job of keeping me warm.

Keeping my chin up was the problem. For one thing, my parents had by now sold both their business and their home in New Jersey, and though my mother reassured me that she would accompany me for surgeries, I nonetheless found their move to Florida unsettling. It was decided that I would move in with Aunt Rose.

I knew that my stays in hospital would be relatively brief, but I did not look forward to the pain. I had had my fill of pain, and the prospect of more filled me with dread. Family photographs taken of me in my room at Mass General show a young woman who has been through a lot of physical and emotional pain, facing the prospect of more. I had had so many operations by that point. How many more, I wondered, could I take? Still, in Dr. Constable I had a world-renowned plastic surgeon. He would be my Geppetto.

I remember the elaborate signing-in procedure as we entered Mass General—like my first day at college. My room was pleasant, with a view of the hospital entrance, and I came to embrace this hope: that I would walk out that door repeatedly in the years ahead, each time looking, feeling, and managing better than when I walked in.

An entourage of doctors and nurses swept into my room. They discussed my facial and hand surgeries, explained how they would take a skin graft from my upper arm—the closest match to my facial skin—and rebuild my lip and chin. Then they would harvest skin from my stomach and add it to my hand, enabling, by degrees, use of my left thumb. Listening to all this, you would think they were talking about a piece of furniture. Carve the wood here, chisel there. Shave a little here, put some veneer there.

The night before my first surgery, I wrote a poem called "Master Builder" and stored it with the others in my journal. It read, in part,

> *knead me,*
> *press me,*
> *mold me . . .*
> *take your mallet*
> *and pound this foot flat again . . .*
> *turn up the corners of this*
> *mouth that has to smile*
> *every now and then*
> *to keep me going on . . .*

The master builders would do a nice job of kneading, pressing, and molding me—my face and hand, to start with. The new lower lip was a welcome addition, for it meant I could drink or eat without risk of spilling anything like a Gerber baby.

Following plastic surgery on my chin, I was fitted with a Jobst chin mask so the new skin would stay flat, with minimal scarring. I was to wear the mask in the evening and at night during sleep. It gave me the look of a bruising hockey player, but it seemed a small price to pay, knowing the scarring would fade.

Next, my index finger and thumb had pins inserted in them to keep them straight. This was the first of six surgeries on that hand. Bandages covered the skin grafts on the thumb and top of my hand, and I would not know until the following week—when the pins were removed—whether I'd have use of the hand. I will never forget Dr. Constable's humble words as I left the hospital after that first surgery. "Carole," he said, "thank you for allowing me to be part of your reconstructive team."

But I was the one to be thankful. Geppetto and his team had gotten off to a wonderful start. I returned a week later to have the pins removed and joked with my doctors that while the protruding pins had been useful against criminals, I was happy to see the end of them. I was overjoyed to see that I could bring my index finger and thumb together. Parents will tell you that one of the markers of a growing infant is that moment when the baby is able to deftly pick up a small object by deploying thumb and forefinger. I had lost that ability, and now I had it back. I would practice picking up items over and over again—a fork, a button, a pen. I pinched myself to be sure this was really true.

With my newfound talent I could cut my own food, hold on to a steering wheel, cinch up a girth, hold a bridle, maybe even play the piano again. Why, I could even type my poems. What's more, to keep occupied, I took up stringing beads. The sheer joy I felt in gaining these two fingers back was inexplicable. As that line from the old Joni Mitchell song says, we don't know what we have till it's gone.

Dr. Constable suggested several months of physical therapy for my hand, but I had already decided on my own brand of physical therapy—a guitar. I had always wanted to play, and with plenty of time on my hands, now was the perfect opportunity to learn and stretch my fingers at the same time. My other self-prescribed therapy, horseback riding, continued to strengthen my hands as I gripped the reins, put the bit in the horse's mouth, or groomed him.

My mother and I celebrated my new fingers and hands by treating ourselves to a clam chowder and lobster dinner at Boston's famous Union Oyster House, built in 1826 and touted as the oldest restaurant in the country. We then shopped for a warm denim jacket, and there were tears streaming down my face when I was able to get my hand through the sleeve. Finally, we went to a music store, and I bought an acoustic six-string Yamaha guitar with a case and beginner's handbook. Linda Ronstadt would no doubt be pleased to know that I would henceforth play and sing duets with her.

8

The Long Haul Back

IN A MATTER OF MONTHS I would mark my thirtieth birthday: February 24, 1977. That I was now bunking in my aunt's spare room said much about the uncertainty in my life. There was no permanence, no regularity or routine, no sense at all of settling into something. I had no prospects—for work, for a mate, even for a place to live. I could look no further ahead than the many operations and recovery periods that Mass General had in store for me. What I had, once again, was time on my hands. And I tried to spend it wisely, even selflessly.

Harry Gaynor, founder of the National Burn Victim Foundation, called and suggested I join this active and supportive group. Invited to a picnic lunch not far from Teaneck, my father and I listened to the wrenching stories of burn victims who faced long periods in hospital, reconstructive surgery, loss of work, and financial worries. I couldn't stay long, for I was wilting from summer humidity in that Jobst bodysuit. (I looked like Batwoman and felt like a diver in a wetsuit during a heat wave. The thing was dreadfully uncomfortable, and zippered, so I could not don it alone.)

While I was at the picnic, Harry Gaynor enlisted my help with a severely burned Puerto Rican man who lived not far from my aunt's place. The man had suffered second- and third-degree burns over his face and upper body while lighting a barbecue grill. When Harry discovered that I spoke Spanish, he asked if I would visit Eduardo Gomez in Hackensack Hospital and help interpret.

No prisoner wants to go back to jail, and that's how returning to that hospital seemed to me. Harry countered, suggesting that the best thing for me was to shift the focus off my own pain and on to helping others. He was right. Working with a burn victim would become a fulfilling experience for me, and I like to think that Eduardo benefited from my counsel and deeply felt compassion.

At Hackensack I introduced myself to Eduardo, told him of my own injuries, and then considered his. He would be terribly disfigured, physically and probably emotionally, for the rest of his life. His brown eyes filling with tears, he asked me if I had wanted to die when I was enduring all the pain. I told him I did, that I had expressed that wish many times—until I found reasons to live. Eduardo told me he had a wife and two young children who depended on him for a living, meager though it was. Those are your reasons to live, I told him. I urged him to work hard in physical therapy and assured him that he would improve steadily, daily.

I thought of Eduardo's circumstances and compared them to mine. How fortunate I was that my medical insurance covered nearly everything, and that the elementary school where I worked had even offered me a monthly stipend. After eight weeks, Eduardo finally left for home. Before he did, I hugged him gently. I wept, and he wept, and we just stared into each other's eyes. We shared something deeper than words: love for a fellow human.

After that visit my attitude started to change. My eyes were opening to a world outside my pain. I made plans to have balloons, flowers, and a cake delivered to Eduardo's house for his homecoming. The note on the flowers read, "De tu amiga que tambien paso por fuego, Carole. Que mantengas tu coraje." ("From your friend in flames, Carole. Be strong.")

Eduardo would be followed by other contacts, all arranged by Harry Gaynor. Among them: Conchita, a three-year-old girl who was scalded when she pulled down a pot of boiling water from the stove; Jose, a man in his twenties with acid burns on his face, neck, and arms; and Rose, a year-old baby girl who had been immersed in a bathtub of scalding water.

Harry kept tapping me on the arm, and it seems I could not refuse him. When I met him, he was a tall, athletic man in his midfifties who kept trim playing tennis. Harry was strong and sturdy, with broad shoulders, but what set him apart was his tireless spirit: he was, and is, among the most giving and generous men I have ever met—a male Mother Teresa.

I would tell people about Harry and the National Burn Victim Foundation, and they would assume that Harry himself had been burned. They were wrong. Harry told me that in 1944 he was in the Allied Air Force, and his plane was shot down over Romania. He was taken as a prisoner of war and fought with the Russians against the Germans. When he thought he was going to die, he made a promise to God (he is a Protestant Christian) that if he was spared, he would make a difference and commit the rest of his life to helping people.

After the war, he made good on that promise and devoted himself to public work: taking kids off the street, heading the March of Dimes, becoming the mayor of South Plainfield, New Jersey. Later, when he was in the business of smoke detection systems, he was touched by contact with burn victims—a woman isolated by virtue of her disfigurement and a family who perished from smoke inhalation. In 1974, he launched the National Burn Victim Foundation from his dining-room table.

The foundation started burn awareness and prevention programs, sent teddy bears to burned children, and set up an emergency burn referral service, a disaster response system (helicopters for transporting patients to burn centers), burn counseling, and much more. Harry raised a million dollars for one burn center, became an expert witness at trials, and had a profound impact on burn victims and their families—including yours truly.

One day Harry invited me to a charity basketball game at the Meadowlands featuring the legendary Bill Bradley, with proceeds to the National Burn Victim Foundation. They already had their "poster child," but they needed an adult burn victim to address the crowd.

"Me?" I told Harry. "Get up in front of thousands of people and speak? In my hideous condition?" I assured him I was no guest speaker.

"You are a teacher," he began, smoothly, persuasively, "and a wonderful example of courage. Put your own feelings aside and think about all the money we can collect for a helicopter to fly burn patients and their families to the right facilities. Think of all the good you will do by speaking."

I finally relented. On a cool, starry evening I went to the arena and gave my brief—but by all accounts, poignant—speech. Still, I declined the photo session that followed, for I wanted no reminders of my tormented condition.

The photographer would later introduce himself to me as Scott Whitehill, and he would become my first romance after the accident. A professional freelance photographer and close to me in age, he had graduated from the Pratt Institute of Arts in New York City. We discovered we had a mutual friend, and I warmed to his unconventionality and unpretentious tastes. He typically wore a turtleneck sweater or crew neck under a sports jacket. It was, or so it seemed to me, the avant-garde look of an artist—one who ate ice cream out of a carton and lived in his late parents' New York City apartment with triple locks on the door.

Even his offer of a date was unconventional. Would I, he asked, join him for a Sunday drive in Central Park, followed by a visit to an elderly woman who was once his nanny? Surprised by the attention of any man, I hesitated but then agreed. I wondered what he saw in me. I could hardly bear to look at myself in the mirror, let alone have a man look at me. I dared not allow myself to fall in love with someone, for I was certain that my love would never be reciprocated. I even began to wonder if our mutual friend had put Scott up to this, out of pity or as a favor.

Still, the Sunday "date" was a breeze. Scott was a born raconteur and easy to be with. We would see each other again.

The phone rang, and on the other end was Melly, concern in his voice. He explained that Bailey had been kicked by another horse while turned out in a paddock for exercise. Low horse on the dominance scale (each herd has an "alpha" horse, with the others falling into place behind that gelding or mare), Bailey was always submissive. But he had gotten too close to the dominant horse's hay, and had received a reprimand from him. The blow to his rump had opened up a wound, and Melly thought the vet should stitch it up.

I arrived at the stable just as the veterinarian pulled up. Melly had Bailey in his stall, and I brought him out, though I was sickened at the sight of the wound. As I held the lead rope while the vet administered a shot of anesthetic to the area, Melly asked the vet if he needed a twitch. (A twitch is a wooden stick with a looped cord on the end of it. The cord can be twisted on the upper lip of the horse to distract him from pain and keep him still.) But the vet deemed it unnecessary and sutured the gash.

I was the one who needed twitching! At the mere whiff of the Betadine and the sight of the stitching, I passed out. How ironic, with all I had been through, that I fainted at the sight of a minor medical procedure.

The tables had turned. Bailey, faithful trustworthy Bailey, had been my physical therapist and buddy all rolled into one. And now Bailey needed me to take care of him. For several weeks I made daily trips to wash the wound and keep it clean with Betadine. I applied fly spray to keep bugs off the wound, I gave him bute (short for phenylbutazone, an anti-inflammatory) tablets crushed in applesauce, to reduce the pain and swelling, and I hand-walked and grazed him. It was good medicine to put this horse's needs ahead of my own—good medicine, and good discipline.

⁂

That fall I went south to visit my parents in their new condo near Fort Lauderdale. I stepped off the plane and into the wheelchair they had waiting for me, looking like a soldier returning from war. My hair had started to grow back, so my crew cut no doubt added to the military look. My body was encased in the sleeveless Jobst bodysuit, my left arm in a sling, my lower face and hand lightly bandaged.

My mother gave me a wide-brimmed hat to shade my face from the sun, and my father showed me a picture of his boat, the *Miss Jene II*. We were going fishing.

Some days the ocean was as flat as a lake on a windless day. Other days, there was a fury about the sea. I loved both moods, for I love water and was born under the astrological sign of Pisces, the fish. My father's favorite stories were set on the water—the time Aunt Molly accidentally sat in a smelly bucket of chum (baitfish), and no one would go near her. The time Dad struck an uncharted reef and had to call the Coast Guard for help. The "May Day! May Day!" seemed comical only in retrospect.

He loved his boat. It was his pride and joy. Shortly after selling the *Miss Jene II,* he had a massive stroke that left him paralyzed and unable to speak. It was as if losing the boat and time on the ocean took his breath away. Like my father, I loved every facet of fishing: the waiting, the baiting, the thrill of catching a fish. Bringing in a hundred-pound tuna may require an hour of work, not to mention great skill. I loved what follows: the cleaning, the cooking. I loved being on the water, the golden light sparkling on the sea, the raucous sound of seagulls, the smell of salt, the sight of humpback whales and porpoises. You never knew what you were going to catch on the ocean—sand sharks, haddock, cod, bluefish, grouper, sea bass. It was part of the great attraction of the sea, not knowing what you had on your line.

The ocean exerted a powerful tug on my father, as it still does on me. The next best thing to riding a horse is to be in a boat on the open sea with a fishing rod in hand. The pungent smell of salt water, the light rocking motion of the boat, the warmth of the Florida sun: it was, and is, intoxicating. We caught several grouper that week. Mom was conscripted to fillet them, and I was given the task of cooking fish dinners back at the condo. The baby grand piano also got some work that week, as I continued to stretch my fingers.

Back up north, Don Goldman suggested respite of another sort. A friend of his owned a cabin near Mount Snow, Vermont; he would ski with his pal, and I would read by the fire. As we approached Brattleboro, Vermont, from Interstate 91, the velvet Green Mountains, almost covered in snow, seemed to beckon. I immediately felt the pull—of good air, a simpler life, a slower pace. The quiet and natural beauty of the area seemed so inviting, and it occurred to me that Bailey would like it there, too—large pastures, trails through the woods. I was also taken in by the charm and history of the town common in Brattleboro, the general store and covered bridges. I thought, It must have been like this a hundred years ago. I could picture horses pulling carriages through those bridges.

The pace of a walking horse had new appeal now. I had slowed down so much myself that the word *hurry* had disappeared from my vocabulary. And by walking more slowly, I learned a valuable lesson. I had lived life as if it were a race, lying in bed with the next fifty chores running through my mind, taking each day on the fly, never hearing the reply when I asked, "How are you?" Now I treasured gazing at the fading sun, listening to the rhythm of rain on a tin roof, following a butterfly's erratic flight. Life for me now was a slow dance, both by necessity and inclination. The tranquillity and beauty of the countryside I would have appreciated anyway, but now they seemed crucial to the long healing process ahead.

The point was underlined when it came time to ponder my future in teaching. Teachers and coworkers back at Washington Elementary School in Union City, New Jersey, had been beseeching me to return for a visit, something I had been putting off. The day of my visit, the city seemed dirtier, noisier, and more crowded than I remembered it from a year ago. It took me fifteen minutes to find a parking space near the school. Hobbling up the stairs and into the principal's office winded me. The principal and his secretary were delighted to see me and escorted me to the teachers' room, where I got a mixed reception. One colleague hugged me and cried, proclaiming it a miracle that I was still alive. Other teachers stole looks or glanced away.

Kids in the hall were ill equipped to face a burn victim. Some pointed and whispered as they passed. Others unleashed questions, unaware that they should politely censor their curiosity and commentary.

"Does it hurt much?"

"Did you get many needles?"

"Man, fire makes you ugly!"

"You look funny."

I retreated as best I could. The truth was, I *did* feel repulsive. Ugly to the bone. People looked at me with pity, and the last thing I wanted was pity. My burned skin and twisted fingers, feet, and toes made me feel like a freak, with a freak's paranoia. Everyone who joked was joking about me. People looked away quickly when they saw me; how different from the long, admiring looks I used to get.

A little of that lingers, even now, twenty-eight years later. All the years have mellowed my crimson scars, but I remember too well what it felt like to be a beauty in her prime one minute, and damaged goods on show the next.

＊　　＊　　＊

In the months and years to follow, surgeons continued their work of overhaul. I was a car on a hoist, but it seemed like every time that once battered and sputtering vehicle was driven home afterward, it ran and looked a little better than before.

During all this time, Geppetto and his helpers at Mass General (doctors Constable and Cohen) were continuing to give my stiff Pinocchio body a little more flex and give. They repeatedly installed pins in my fingers, training the digits to stay erect and stop curling. The pins poked out, as if my flesh were growing metal, and they caught on everything—clothes, upholstery, my own flesh. The pins meant work, since I had to keep them clean using peroxide and Neosporin ointment. The pins also meant pain, for they both restricted my movement and hurt all the time they were in. And if

I dreaded the pins' insertion, I dreaded even more the torture of their removal; that pain put me on the ceiling.

For each operation, my mother flew up from Florida to be at my side. It was as if she were making up for all the lost time she had spent as a working mother. My mother and I fell into a routine of sorts, a routine built around too many medical appointments inked on a calendar. After each operation, we would play tourist, enjoying the historic attractions of Boston and environs—Salem, famous for the witch trials, Longfellow's Wayside Inn, Plymouth Rock, and the statue of Paul Revere on his horse. I had taken a special interest in such statues, and was told that the position of the war hero's horse told the soldier's fate: one foot off the ground, he was wounded; two feet off the ground, he died; all four feet on the ground, he survived the battle.

Months went by, and Pinocchio's face was much improved. I was at first heartbroken when they took off the bandages, and I could see that my chin was still scarred. I jokingly asked Dr. Constable for a facial prosthesis, but he assured me that with time—and the Jobst chin mask—my face would improve. I was expecting the old Carole, but the old Carole never came back. Eventually I decided that the new one was just fine. In fact, I came to like her better for her courage and strength. And after all that surgery on my left hand, it, too, was coming along. Only the left foot remained.

Dr. Constable passed me on to Dr. Edwin Wyman, chief of orthopedic surgery at Mass General. A tall, slender, and distinguished-looking man with steel gray hair, he had been examining my foot, watching me walk, peering over his glasses at me. My mother was looking on, and I dispatched her—I hope not too rudely.

"I would like to see you alone," I told him.

"I was waiting for you to say that," he replied. His manner was direct as he began his assessment. "Carole, there has been a lot of tendon damage to your left foot, and it's now shorter than your right one. The contractures are not allowing you to put your foot flat down, so you walk on the side of it. You have no movement in your left ankle or toes, and little in your right foot as well. I can do a fusion on your ankle, with staples holding it in place, which may enable you to walk with your foot flat on the ground, but the procedure will be irreversible. You will never gain back the motion in your ankles you once had."

Dr. Wyman explained further that following surgery I would wear a cast—with pins in my toes like the ones in my fingers—for six months. The outcome would be clearer after surgery, once the cast came off. Then would begin the uphill climb of physical therapy. "The operation," he said, "is a gamble, but you might be able to walk better than you can now."

My mind was made up. I wasn't going through life limping. When my mother rejoined us, she was both upset at being left out of the equation and miffed by what she took to be Dr. Wyman's dispassionate veneer. She spoke from behind a stubborn jut of jaw: "What do you mean, it's uncertain what the outcome will be?"

No guarantees, he told her.

"Mom," I cut in, "this is my body, and the decision will affect my mobility for the rest of my life. I'm going to take that chance and have the fusion. It's my only ticket to being able to walk normally again. My mind's made up."

I was starting to make a lot of decisions, following instincts I did not know I possessed. After we left the hospital, I picked up a newspaper at lunch and glanced at the real estate ads: "Beachfront cottage for rent, monthly, Hyannisport. Call for more info." We drove to the Cape and looked at the charming three-bedroom cottage that overlooked the ocean and the Kennedy compound. I envisioned myself walking daily in the sand on the beach once the cast was off my leg and playing guitar on the large screened porch with its glorious ocean view. Both would be therapeutic in every way. I would be close to Boston, if need be. I could fish, go clamming, swim to my heart's content, go to antiques auctions. My mother, father, brother, and friends could all visit. I secured the cottage. A few things, at least, were falling into place.

The morning of my foot operation, my heart was in my mouth. All the surgeries, all that time in hospital, had not dulled the fear. The pre-op routine, the anesthesia, the gleaming metal and overpowering lights in the operating room—I dreaded every detail, but especially this operation. This one was pivotal. My life's mobility was on the line here.

The previous day I had happened to spend a little time with Alec Robertson, a fifty-something Scotsman in the room next to mine. He was diabetic, legally blind, had had one leg amputated below the knee, and then the other; he was now being fitted for prosthetic legs. A shiver ran down my spine when I saw those stumps. Was this to be my fate too? I had been warned of a worst-case scenario:

loss of limb. To stop my body from trembling, I tried to live by my own rule: Face what you fear. Look the devil in the eye.

My mother remembers what it was like waiting, that day. She would never forget what she called, "the longest eight hours I've ever spent." She recalls that the staff at Mass General were kind and sincere. There was a special waiting room set up, with coffee, sandwiches, and chapels of every denomination alongside. Social workers would come and talk to her. They would telephone down to the operating room for progress reports. My mother remembers crying there alone—the family couldn't afford both parents to be there.

Finally, Dr. Wyman came out in his green scrubs. He kissed my mother on one cheek and told her, "Mom, we made it, and I'm just as happy as you are!" My mother had thought he was insensitive, but she now saw how wrong that assessment had been. Dr. Wyman had been more worried than she was, because he knew what could have happened. He cried, she cried. "There's training and therapy ahead," he told my mother. "It's a long haul back. But I give you my word. She'll be fine now."

Overjoyed and relieved at the outcome, I resolved not to gripe about the lengthy time I'd have to spend in a cast. To remind myself of my good fortune, I asked a nurse to take a photograph of me next to Alec Robertson. The photo shows us both from the hip down. We're in wheelchairs, my wasted and scarred legs set alongside his stumps.

I vowed to look at that photograph every day, especially if I started feeling sorry for myself or began to whine. I at least have my parts, I told myself. They may be charred and scarred, but at least I have them. Later, I had that photo blown up and posted it in the bathroom. While some complained it was grotesque, the photo lifted me, in part because Alec was so irrepressible and such a prankster. (He used a Hamm radio to frighten the night nurse into thinking she was "hearing voices.") A blind and legless man seemed to have kept his high spirits, and damn it, so would I.

9

"It Wasn't Your Fault"

IF I WAS FATED to be burned in the fire, I was also fated to survive and turn to a life with horses. But I would need a kick start to begin building that life, and I got it thanks to a chance encounter.

The years from 1976 through 1979 had been marked by endless rounds of surgery and therapy as doctors in Boston attempted the recasting of Carole Fletcher. But during a visit back to New Jersey in September 1977—long before I found the cottage at Hyannisport—I happened to connect with Don Goldman. He had invited me to accompany him to synagogue for the Jewish High Holy Days. Although I hadn't attended these ceremonies in years, for some reason I decided to go and afterward to break the traditional fast at his parent's home. We were just leaving the temple when a man approached me. He was short and rotund, with a ruddy complexion, small piercing eyes, and a confident swagger.

"Excuse me," he said, his soft voice at odds with his bearing, "my name is Richard Weiner. I don't mean at all to be forward, but

I couldn't help notice your injuries. Was it some sort of accident?" His boldness and frankness took me aback, and I was both embarrassed and emotional in response.

Don's eyes narrowed. "Yes," he said, "she was badly burned in the basement of her house, working on a car." Don then grabbed my hand and started to pull me away.

Weiner must have been used to such rebuffs. He offered a bland smile. "The reason I ask," he said, "is I'm a lawyer, and if you wouldn't mind, I'd like to talk to you about the accident. There might be some negligence involved." He handed me his card, which I slipped into my pocket, and I thanked him.

To that point I had given no thought to how the accident had happened—only to recovering from it. But this lawyer now prompted me to give it some thought. Just how *did* the accident happen? I took out the calling card and just stared at it: "Richard Weiner, Attorney. Accidents, Products Liability and Negligence."

The old Porsche sat in the garage of my Aunt Rose's apartment building—home for the time being. I hadn't driven the car in more than a year, but one day something compelled me to get behind the wheel. It was a beauty, with classic touches—wooden dashboard and steering wheel. After a few minutes in the parking lot to get the feel of this powerful machine, I mustered the courage to drive it on the street. I had in mind a certain destination: Richard Weiner's office.

The building was old but comfortable, and I hobbled into the office bearing his name. The receptionist asked me if I had an appointment, and though I said no, she did buzz Mr. Weiner to let him know I was there. Immediately he opened his office door and welcomed me in.

"Mr. Weiner," I started stammering, "I never considered how the accident happened. But now I'm curious."

He scanned me up and down, arms crossed. He asked how many operations I had had and how many more I could expect. Had anyone been in the house prior to the accident? Any repairmen, for example? Had the landlord contacted me since the accident? Did I have the rental lease agreement? How, to the best of my recollection, had the accident happened? His most surprising question hit me like a wrecking ball: Did I intend for the accident to happen? I started to laugh, thinking that the man before me was certifiably insane. Who in her right mind would ever put herself through such pain as I had endured?

"I had to ask you," he explained apologetically. Then he said, "With your permission, I'd like to investigate your accident. There could be some negligence that contributed to the accident. It won't cost you a nickel for me to investigate, and if I litigate, it will be done on a contingency basis."

I signed the necessary papers, and the following day Richard Weiner launched his investigation into the explosion. On the way home from his office, I considered driving past my old house but decided against it. Curiosity had brought me to the lawyer's office but would take me no further. Not enough remained to get me close to that house on Kinderkamack Road.

One day I returned to my aunt's high-rise to find a message from Richard Weiner. My attorney seemed anxious to see me, and a few days later I drove the Porsche, cast and all, to see him.

I opened his office door and saw him standing, looking out the window, while the sun streamed in, a bouquet of flowers on his desk. He turned and walked toward me with a grim smile. "Here," he said, handing me the flowers. "These are for you. I heard the good news about the operation." My years of reconstructive surgery at Massachusetts General had begun, and someone was keeping him appraised of my progress. But his was an awkwardly delivered get-well card; he appeared to be strung tighter than barbed wire.

"Thanks," I replied. "You must have some news for me. Have you found out anything about the accident?"

"Carole," he said, "it wasn't your fault." He looked directly at me. I willed my breathing to be quiet, forcing back tears, clenching my teeth. I couldn't speak; my hands began to quiver, and my face went stiff.

"I visited the scene of the accident," he said, finally putting his cards on the table. "The gasoline-fired explosion is known as a flashback. Fumes from the gasoline were ignited by the pilot light on the water heater. Your landlord informed me that the gas company had been there a couple of days prior to the accident. The manufacturer of the water heater should have had a protective device on it to prevent such flashbacks. Your accident could have been prevented. There is definite negligence and product liability involved here. With your permission, I'd like to begin litigation."

Richard Weiner eyed my cast.

"What part will I have to play?" I asked him.

"You'll have to give depositions under oath to lawyers, and if it goes to trial, you'll have to testify." He straightened the tie at his throat, a gesture that reminded me of Rodney Dangerfield's between-jokes punctuation. But this was no joke.

"And tell about the whole accident and operations over and over again?" I asked. I had visions of endlessly reliving the accident. Worse, I conjured a jury wanting a closer look at my scarred frame.

He was quick to reply.

"Look, Carole. You will never, ever be compensated for the unspeakable pain you've been through and are yet to face. I'm a personal injury lawyer who has represented many people with injuries that don't come close to the magnitude of yours. I've been able to recover substantial amounts for their pain and suffering. While it doesn't erase the pain, it will certainly help make a better life for you."

Loss of mobility, I had read in a newspaper, could be worth thousands of dollars in damages. What fine experts these attorneys must be, I thought, to quantify the cost of pain and suffering. Yet Weiner was right. If he could prove negligence or liability, this case would alter my life.

"All right, Mr. Weiner," I told him, "you can start a lawsuit. Just remember, though, I'm going through enough to get myself back on my feet right now. Spare me as much as you can from your legal entanglements." He was delighted by this news and said he would keep me posted by mail.

True to his word, Richard Weiner did keep me posted. My depositions, he would say later, had "scared the hell out of the defen-

dants." The gas company's records, which my lawyer had subpoe-
naed, contained a discrepancy regarding the dates of the service
calls on the water heater. That's because the pilot light on the heater
was faulty.

The most likely options, he said, were an out-of-court settlement or a jury trial. For the latter, he said he would ask me to wear
a bathing suit and show my injuries. "It will be a cold day in hell,"
I told him, my eyes narrowing as I said it, "before I ever go on display before a jury, no matter how much money it might fetch. Go
for a settlement."

My palms felt damp. Coolly, my lawyer began cleaning a finger-
nail with a paper clip. "Don't think about money," he advised.
"Think about your future."

"With your pocket growing a little fatter because of it!" I
snapped, scarcely believing I had used those words.

He conceded that he would be well paid and predicted the case
would be settled out of court. He stood up, we shook hands, and I
looked past him at the oil paintings on the walls: pastoral scenes.
That's what I had in mind these days, not litigation. A few months
later, I returned from a ride to find a note: "Call your lawyer."

✳ ✳ ✳

Richard Weiner had been negotiating with the gas company, the
maker of the water heater, even the service station that sold me the
gas. He had threatened all of them with legal action. I felt my stomach tighten as I asked, "What was the last offer made?"

"One-point-one million dollars," he replied. "That would be
the largest personal injury amount in the history of New Jersey."

I gasped. My near-death experience was about to make history. The settlement would spare me the ordeal of reliving the fire, and I was not tempted at all by Weiner's remark that a jury might award me three times that amount. Weeks later I picked up the check and made a photocopy of it, for I knew I would never again see a check with so many zeroes on it made out to my name. The settlement brought with it profoundly mixed feelings: my heart told me one thing (you want no part of this), and my head said another (take the money and make a life with horses). The amount of money seemed surreal, but it brought no pleasure or satisfaction and certainly no sense of compensation, only a little relief. For that, at least, I was grateful.

10

Goodbye Bailey, Hello Vermont

SIX MONTHS LATER, the cast came off. No more sponge baths, no more crutches that made me feel like a pig on roller skates, no more snaking a wire hanger down my leg to relieve the awful itching. Still, there remained a cloud of anxiety. How would I walk once the cast and big boot were removed? I looked over at my mother, and it suddenly hit me how much she had aged, what a toll the accident had exacted.

Days before the cast came off, something had changed between us. A truce had been called in an old mother-daughter war. That morning my menstrual cycle—which the trauma of the fire had put on hold all this time—began anew.

"Mom," I said to her, my voice hushed, "I've started my period."

She put her arms around me and began to weep, pain and sorrow written all over her face. "I know I wasn't around when you got your period for the first time, honey. I made a lot of mistakes I wish I could correct. But I'm glad I'm here for you this time around." We held on to each other for a long time, my head resting on her shoulder.

My mother was there when the cast came off, as she had been every step of the way. With his cutter, Dr. Wyman had managed to create two perfect halves, and I pulled my leg free. My bare skin felt odd in the open air and looked much paler than the rest of the leg. Worse, the calf muscle had shrunk so much I wanted to cry. How would I ever leg a horse properly again?

Next the pins were removed, the pins in my toes that had been the bane of my existence. A source of infection, they caught on everything, and I was glad to see the end of them. But their extraction sent pain shooting up my foot, and I almost passed out. The good news came with the X-ray. Dr. Wyman pronounced the operation "a winner!"

With tears in her eyes, my mother extended her hand to the doctor and thanked him, "from the bottom of my heart."

"My reward," he said, "is the smile on your daughter's face. She sure defies all odds."

I took a few steps with a cane, put all my weight on the left foot, and winced at the pain. My mother, though, was encouraged, and her face lit up. "This calls for some new shoes!" she said, ever fashion-conscious. As we passed under the Exit sign at Mass General, I turned back for one last look at the hospital where I'd been reassembled. I was exiting one part of my life and about to begin another.

My first task was to get my body back in some sort of shape, and I knew that beach and sand would get me there. Every morning, clad in leotard and tights to protect me from the sun, I set off barefoot down the beach from the cottage at Hyannisport and planted a flagged marker in the sand before heading back. Every day the marker would be set farther on. I needed to put weight on those legs of mine, and while riding Bailey later on would strengthen my legs, walking on sand was my therapy for the moment. I had December for company now; I had plucked her from the Goldmans, who were sad to see her go.

Under the noon sun, I would swim in the ocean and later rest in the shade of an umbrella. In the early evening I would surf-cast on the sandy flats and inlets for striped bass, cod, or flounder or dig for clams (quahogs were my favorite), then cook the catch of the day—sometimes stuffed clams, sometimes what the locals called "chowdah." I would learn there were a hundred ways to cook a clam. Picking the native beach plum—a fruit that grows on bushes in Cape Cod's sandy soil—and making plum jam, as well as baking, became favorite pastimes. At dusk, I'd pick a few tunes on my guitar to stretch out my fingers and entertain myself.

That summer, a steady flow of guests came to that quaint beach-front house with its weathered gray shingles and white shutters. My family, as well as my boyfriend, Scott Whitehill, the freelance photographer I had met following my address at the charity basketball game in the Meadowlands, and many other friends, stayed for long visits. One friend, Beryl Goldbaum, remembers carrying me into the ocean when I first got the cottage. She would bring me beads to string for necklaces and bracelets, books to read. I grew stronger and, with guests, explored Cape Cod from the tip of Provincetown to the islands of Nantucket and Martha's Vineyard. I happened to meet Edward Kennedy Jr., who worked on the ferry to the islands. He was an inspiration to me, for he had lost his right leg to bone cancer in 1973. By summer's end, I could walk several miles with just the slightest hint of a limp. My hair had grown to shoulder-length and was thicker than before, just as Vincent said it would be. The gleam in my eye had returned, the one that came with confidence.

By the end of August, when the blue skies were beginning to fade, I felt strong and determined to return to my old teaching job. But going back, it turned out, was a mistake. Though the principal had made allowances for me and scheduled all my classes on the first floor to save me having to climb stairs, the joy I had felt when I started teaching fresh out of college had vanished. The hectic pace of the inner city, finding parking, even walking into the school, all drained me. I yearned for a more tranquil setting.

＊　＊　＊

Scanning the *New York Times* one Sunday, a Help Wanted ad caught my eye. The School for International Training (affiliated with the Peace Corps and based in Brattleboro, Vermont) needed someone with a master's degree in education to teach teachers how to teach English as a second language. I sent in a résumé, got an interview, and was told the job was mine if I wanted it.

I sat in a restaurant in Brattleboro overlooking the Connecticut River and admired the rolling mountains while mulling over the offer. Did I want to move here, more than two hundred miles from Teaneck, without knowing a soul? My own family were Floridians now, but I wasn't ready for a hot climate. Dr. Constable had warned me against exposing my skin grafts to the sun. My gait was still clumsy and ungainly, and my teaching schedule at this new job would not, I presumed, tax me physically. I had always, I told myself, made friends wherever I went. I thought of the great peace I had felt while staying at that ski lodge with Don and his pal. That day in Brattleboro I'd seen a T-shirt proclaiming that there were more cows in Vermont than people (the state population was then half a million). That curious fact appealed to me. I took the job.

My father, and especially my mother—who seemed impressed that her daughter would be what she called "a college professor"—heartily approved, as did Scott. I had continued to see him, and we had formed an attachment, but if he would eventually become keen on moving with me to Vermont, he wasn't at first.

"You're moving to *Vermont?*" he asked, incredulous. "That's nowhere's land!"

"Scott, I'm going on with my life," I told him. "I've got a great job offer. Here's a chance of a lifetime to move somewhere of *my* choice, where I'll be happy. Besides," I added, "I'm not a city person anymore. Never really was."

There was a pause. He stroked his beard, inhaled deeply, and then announced that he, too, would move to Vermont. We talked a little more and then agreed to rent a small house somewhere, a place in the country with room for Bailey and December.

The dream of country living in Vermont did not unfold quite as I imagined it. Scott and I found a place all right: a rented white clapboard house in historic Westmoreland, New Hampshire, just a few miles across the Connecticut River from Vermont. Established in 1735, the town was originally known as Great Meadows and was part of a line of fort towns built along the river to protect pioneers from the Indians. Cleared of its tall pines, oaks, and maples, the rolling land that rose from the fertile river valley offered fine pastures for dairy cattle and for growing corn. Set up on a knoll, the rental house lorded over seven acres of lush grass dotted with wildflowers and a small barn that had once housed chickens.

Right after my lawsuit had been settled and the amount of my compensation had become clear, my father came for a visit, and my boyfriend arranged a welcoming party on our newly built deck, with catered food and drinks, flowers, and a bluegrass band he'd hired from Boston.

When the last guests had trickled away, and Dad had gone to bed, Scott sat me down on the deck, the glow of the candles flickering next to us. He took both of my hands in his and told me he had been waiting a long time to ask me something. "Will you marry me?"

I let the question hang for a while. The June night air was cool, and I started to shiver. I had had too many glasses of wine, and I told Scott I would sleep on it.

Next morning, I sought my father's counsel. We went out for a ride, me on my horse Angel Babe, my father on a borrowed quarter horse named Rio. It was a beautiful day, the meadows peppered with dandelions and bluets. "I can understand why you like it here," my father said as we rode. "This is God's country."

When I told him about Scott's proposal, my father wasn't surprised. "The minute you get a sizable settlement," he said, "Scott asks you to marry him. Not very hard to figure out, is it?" I hadn't seen the handwriting on the wall, nor had I ever heard from Scott the word *love*. I was choked up with emotion and couldn't respond to what my father had said. I had made two bad decisions about marriage in my younger days, and I was not about to make a third. It was painfully clear to me that Scott was a gold digger. My father's advice was gently but firmly delivered.

"It's time," my father told me, "to take off the blinders, sweetie. Better to be hurt a little now than a whole lot later." It was good advice, and I followed it.

*　　　　　　*　　　　*　　　　*

My new life in the New England countryside marked a true departure from everything I had always known. Even my life with horses took momentous twists.

Throughout the years of reconstructive surgery at Mass General, I had continued to ride Bailey for physical and psychological therapy—even while I spent the six months with a cast on my left leg. The first time I rode in that cast, Melly gave me a hand.

"With that plaster on," he said with a wink, "that horse is gonna think he's got Mama Cass sitting on top of him," referring to the portly singer in the then popular group the Mamas and the Papas.

"So call me Mama Cast," I retorted. And he did.

Owing to the cast, I had to mount Bailey from the "off" side, the right side. Not all horses are happy to be mounted in this unusual way, but Bailey obliged. He turned his head toward my stirrup, sniffed, then gazed at my foot. It was a gaze that reflected years of patiently teaching many people to ride. True, age had taken away some of his muscle tone, but it hadn't lessened his ability to instill confidence in his rider.

The snag was that left leg. No stirrup would accommodate the big boot at the end of it, so my leg just hung against the side of my horse. I nudged Bailey forward and he moved right off without hesitation. My eyes were cast downward, looking for expression in his ears and eyes. Bailey walked deliberately on, but I sensed he knew he was carrying fragile baggage. Within half an hour, we were circling, turning, backing, and making figure eights, as if we were dance partners. I took him up to a jog, feeling tight at first, then relaxing and enjoying this moment of sweet perfect harmony with my horse.

Back on the ground, I could feel the ache in my thighs. Muscles I hadn't used in a while made their complaints known. Still, I relished the exhilaration of that ride and tossed my pain to the wind.

"Sore?" Melly asked, grinning up at me with the sun in his eyes.

"Piece of cake," I replied, returning his wink of an hour before and poking a crutch tip at him. It had felt so good to be moving quickly and adroitly on Bailey, to feel that rush of wind on my face, to be so mobile while still encased in a heavy plaster cast. It also gave me great comfort to know that I had such a forgiving horse. I owed Bailey's Irish Cream a lot.

One day at Mar-Bel's, as I rubbed his neck and talked to him gently, offering him carrots all the while, I was hit by a stark realization. Here I was, planning on moving a few hundred miles away, and I didn't have a truck or horse trailer to haul Bailey. A chapter of my life was closing, and perhaps my life with Bailey as well. He was, after all, a horse with some age on him: he was closing in on twenty. In my new life, maybe I needed a challenging horse, not a "made" horse like Bailey. But the thought of life without Bailey created a dull, sinking feeling in my chest.

Then I thought of my friend Rita, whose daughter Nancy adored Bailey. She was always asking me if she could ride him. Mother and daughter had been looking for a horse but hadn't found one, and in my heart I knew Bailey would be the perfect match for her. An eleven-year-old girl to kiss his nose every day, to ride him and bring him sacks of carrots—Bailey would be in horse heaven, and he could stay right here at Melly's. A move is hard on an old horse, and he'd called Mar-Bel's home for many years.

Bailey had been there when I needed him most. "He Will Carry You," my mother had written on that poster, and indeed he had. My mother was right: in time, I believe I *did* become more beautiful on the inside. I learned something important about my changed appearance—that appearance is superficial, just a veneer. I learned the true meaning of beauty. Beauty is wisdom, what we do, how we treat others. It is the love we give. Horses know this; Bailey certainly did. I never met a horse with a face-lift yet, or a horse impressed by one.

That day I left the stable feeling a great sense of loss. "Goodbye, Bailey" were words I found hard to think or say, yet I had become convinced that this was how it should be. In his golden years, my golden horse would take on one last job—fulfilling an innocent child's dreams. I felt certain that some seal had been set on all that had happened, and it was time to move on.

I made another decision around this time: I gave away the '53 Porsche Super Coupe to a friend. Another kind of horsepower was calling to me, and that car wasn't much good for hauling hay or grain.

11

Instant Chemistry

ONE WARM SPRING evening in 1977, I journeyed with friends to a horse auction where I encountered both a trickhorse and a trick-horse trainer.

Our destination that day was Crowley's Auction and Horse Sales in Agawam, Massachusetts. It wasn't far (I had just taken possession of the beachfront cottage), and I'd be helping out a friend who sought a bombproof horse for her young daughter. Horse auctions, I knew, are not the best place to look. They're often dumping grounds for unsound horses or ones with incurable habits, or, worse, for outlaws. But sometimes an owner with too many horses cannot keep a family pet, an honest citizen. As always with horses, it's buyer beware, but sometimes a good one will come up for sale at auction. Such was our hope that day.

Horse trailers and hefty pickup trucks dotted the grounds, and we could hear the horsemen and horsewomen—sometimes as they leaned into the beds of their trucks—holding forth on the state of the equine economy. The term *horse-poor* is rooted in a hard truth: Many people with get-rich-quick ideas built on horses discover that get-poor-quick is the more likely outcome.

That day, the pens and stalls were filled with all sorts of horses and ponies. They waited in readiness to be ridden or led by hand through a narrow alley and into the ring. There each horse stayed until the gavel came down and the auctioneer proclaimed the gelding, mare, or stallion "Sold!" to the highest bidder. We saw chestnuts, sorrels, bays, grays, blacks, and a palomino and pinto or two. Their states told their stories: Some were fat, groomed, and polished. Some desperately needed more food. Others were banged and bruised after claustrophobic trips in crude livestock trailers. Then there were the renegades who bore the scars of their mistreatment and who defended themselves the only way they knew: by baring teeth or kicking at any human who came near.

A few lucky ones could anticipate rehab in good homes where a horse-keen child or adult would dote on them. Some would go to a horse dealer who would train them for a short time and sell them for quick profit. But auctions also draw the slaughterers, like vultures, who would turn horseflesh into pet food. I always knew the price of horse meat was high when the "killers" gathered in numbers at a horse auction. For many horses, auction is the last stop.

We scanned the pens looking for a medium-sized horse with kind eyes. A steel gray Appaloosa with a flashy blanket over his hindquarters stood quietly, head low, almost asleep. He caught my attention. His pen was clean, with an empty feed bucket and full water pail, and flakes of green timothy and clover hay were set in one corner. My friend approached him, and he came over immediately, nickering softly. We were told he belonged to a known horse trader at the auction, a man from Avon, Connecticut, named Larry Gagnon.

Horse traders are sometimes called "manure spreaders," and this one was something of a legend around there. People said he looked like a character out of a B western, with the rough-hewn style of a gunslinger from the Old West. Larry Gagnon was the genuine article—a cowboy who had spent his youth working on his uncle's ranch in Montana. When he joined his family back east, he started a boarding stable and then shod and sold horses, many of them straight from Crowley's Auction.

Gagnon had also trained a few trick horses and bore the moniker "the Frontiersman." He even had his own television series out of Hartford for a while. The horse world is rife with rumor, and word was Larry Gagnon had a weakness for palomino horses and pretty women.

We sat through the auction, sipping our Cokes and waiting for the gray Appy. As the auctioneer announced the arrival of each horse, that horse drew all eyes. Accustomed to familiar surroundings, the freedom of the pasture, and a few known handlers, accustomed, above all, to routine, some horses sent to auction dance or rear in panic. There are no dull moments at these events. Finally, a pretty brunette in her thirties rode in on the gray Appaloosa while a burly man with a booming voice touted the horse's virtues.

This was Larry Gagnon. I studied his weathered face and brawny build. With strong hands and big bones, he was a man built for work. Though he must have been pushing sixty, he had an intimidating presence. Larry Gagnon dressed western—wide-brimmed straw cowboy hat, open-necked Rockmount shirt with snaps for buttons, belt buckle the size of a dinner plate in Wrangler jeans that bunched over his Justin boots. Genuine cowboy boots.

The boots of a born promoter. Gagnon smothered people with broad smiles and aggressive fast talk. Keenly aware that Crowley's had its share of deal makers and fat wallets, Gagnon walked the ring with an awkward, bowlegged gait and assumed the plain manner of a farmhand. "Now look here, folks," he crowed, "this here is the *best* Appaloosa [Apple-ooza, he pronounced it] to ever come through this auction. So dead-broke Grandma can ride him! You're missing out on this one, folks. Dig a little deeper into them wallets, and he can be yours. You won't get 'wallet whiplash' on this one!"

The miked auctioneer moved the bidding along, then paused, theatrically, to ask Gagnon, "Hey, Larry, does this horse do any tricks?"

With the style and timing of a stand-up comic, Gagnon took his cue. "Yeah, he does tricks all right. He tricks me into thinking I should feed him twice a day! What, you want tricks? It'll cost you extra!" Howls of laughter greeted this performance.

"Look here, folks," Gagnon went on, "this horse rides the best and is as flashy as I've ever had." (Later I would hear him say much the same about every horse he was selling.)

The bidding continued, but not to Gagnon's liking, for he scorned the final offer, saying he'd take the gelding back home before accepting that insulting price. My friend was intrigued, and we later sought out the big man to ask if we could see the horse another time at his barn. We had spotted Gagnon sitting on hay bales, and when he rose to his full height, I put him at just over six feet. Up close he looked more and more like John Wayne. In the course of conversation, he offered my friend a bone-crushing handshake and a tooth-rattling backslap. Then he handed her a card and advised calling first, since he was often away doing Wild West shows.

He cast a glance at me with my cane. "Looks like trouble found you, darlin'," he said. "Here's my card if you ever need a horse, though by your looks you're in no shape for one now." I let his barb slide. He wasn't interested in hearing about me, only in a sale. I wondered aloud if he had any literature on his trick horses.

"Course I do, sweetheart," he cooed, then shuffled through some papers before handing me a photo of himself standing with a broad smile while beside him—sitting, like an attentive dog beside his master—was a flashy palomino. This was no dog, but a Trigger lookalike with trickster smarts. The eight-by-ten glossy was signed, "The Frontiersman and Wolf." He suggested I put it up on my wall, that it "might be valuable someday!"

I looked down at the photo, at the handsome palomino with the flowing mane. Ever since I was a child trying to teach tricks to my own pets in the basement at home in Teaneck, I had wondered how it was done. How *did* Trigger learn to nod his head and tell Roy which card to play in those westerns? It struck me that Larry Gagnon might have some answers to that question, and I made plans to see him perform a few weeks later at the Hebron Fair in Connecticut.

To that fair went the same threesome: my friend Beth, her daughter, and me. After our fill of fair food—sausage with peppers and onions, french fries, funnel cakes—we drifted over to the ring where Gagnon and his trick horse Wolf were to perform. Accompanied by circus music, Gagnon rode in at a gallop, his horse big and yellow, golden mane flying, the rider in a red satin shirt, white fringe swaying. This man loved the spotlight.

Phase one of his show was a sharpshooting and whip act. With the pretty brunette from the auction ring acting as Gagnon's accomplice, and never losing that brilliant smile, they pulled off some of the classics: Gagnon shooting at a handheld target behind him using only a mirror as guide, then deploying a bullwhip to pluck a cigarette from a cowgirl's mouth.

But it was as the Frontiersman, alone in the ring with his horse (not Wolf that day, but a quarter horse palomino stallion named Gentry), that Larry Gagnon captured people's hearts. I was completely mesmerized. In a melodramatic voice, the announcer told the story of a cowboy out on the range who had been forced, tragically, to shoot his own beloved horse. But the horse had defied all odds and come back to life. This same horse would later kneel, lie down, stand on a pedestal, and—this was Gagnon's signature pose—sit up while his rider stood on the saddle, one arm up in the air and the other holding the reins.

What made this spectacle so endearing to the audience was not the horse's size or breeding. It was the partnership between human and horse. I remember thinking that this unique communication, on the ground and in the saddle, must be the ultimate form of riding and training. Here was a man who seemed to regard his horse not in utilitarian terms, but as a close friend. Turns out I was wrong about Larry Gagnon as a horse gentler (someone who uses persuasion, not force, to school a young or untrained horse). But I would find that out later for myself.

A teacher, I instinctively went to the library to learn about teaching horses tricks. I came up empty-handed, as I did at the bookstore. All I could find was *The Art of Horsemanship,* written by a Greek cavalry officer named Xenophon three hundred years before the birth of Christ. Xenophon knew, even then, about treating horses with kindness and the power of the carrot.

※　　　※　　　※

The trick horse and my life as a trick-horse trainer were far down the road. It was 1978, I was thirty-one years old, and I had no horse to train or even a decent place to put him if I had one.

Home then was that rented house in Westmoreland, New Hampshire. An easy and pleasant drive took me from the property to my job at the School for International Training in Brattleboro, Vermont, where I taught teachers the skills they would need to teach English as a second language in inner cities. I was walking with a slight limp, but my schedule was not onerous. And while my left hand needed more surgery, it was at least functional.

I was also settling nicely into the New England countryside. Left behind were asphalt and exhaust fumes, triple locks on apartment doors and concern for personal safety. Here, if you heard a gunshot, it was a hunter. People in small rural places, I would discover, didn't lock their doors; they left keys in cars, and helped their neighbors. Many years later, in 2003, I happened to be reading a magazine and spotted something called the State of Caring Index, compiled by the United Way. The organization had ranked states in the union based on economic and financial well-being and levels of education, health, volunteerism, charity, civic engagement, safety, and protection of the environment. The top ten "caring" states were northern states, with New Hampshire a sterling second and every New England state not far behind. The bottom ten were all southern states, with Louisiana last. "The warm north," the magazine headline had read, "the chilly south."

I loved the quiet in New Hampshire and took sustenance from it. I'd go on long drives, with December riding shotgun, her chin resting on the rolled-down window as she surveyed the passing hills, the historic houses, the covered bridges. The only thing missing was a horse in my barn.

Missing Bailey terribly, I cleaned out the barn, made one stall ready, set out my tack, and went looking. Desperation may have clouded my judgment, for I ended up with a seven-year-old mare, a dish-faced sorrel pinto out of a quarter horse mare by a local Arabian stallion. She had a fine luster to her coat and was a good size for me, 14.3 hands. How could I go wrong, I told myself, with a name like Angel Babe?

But this mare was more babe than angel. When she was in heat, she was ornery. High-strung and independent, she wasn't people-friendly like Bailey. I never did warm up to her, nor she to me. She spooked at loud trucks, bolted past cows, and when we chanced on deer out on the trail, she'd wheel around and try to run, her flight instinct kicking into high gear. Nevertheless, we hacked everywhere, through meadows resplendent with lady's slippers, jack-in-the-pulpit, and other wildflowers, and along bridle paths in the woods till the last light of the sun faded from the hills.

But the house on the hill and the marish mare were mere stepping stones to something grander—Singin' Saddles Ranch, my own version of Gene Autry's Melody Ranch.

※　　　　※　　　　※

The hunt for horses became a hunt for land. One day, after looking over an old cattle farm for sale, my father and I stopped for a meal at the Sunshine Restaurant, just down the road from my rented place in Westmoreland. There we chatted with a neighbor, Rick Goodnow, an excavator who was selling a forty-five-acre piece on the other side of town.

Dad and I wasted no time in walking the land—rugged woods with an exquisite stand of oak and maple and an income-producing gravel bank in one corner. Stone walls separated sections of erstwhile pasture now overgrown with trees. The rolling land had a peaceful, bucolic feel to it, with its wild blackberries, blueberry bushes, and apple trees. Set back from the paved road, it afforded complete privacy yet remained accessible. We walked through the woods to a spot where any observer looking closely through the trees was rewarded with stunning and panoramic views of the rolling hills beyond. What a place for a house, I thought. An old trailer on the property offered a prospective buyer temporary abode, and the woods were rich in bridle paths for riding. A woman and her horse could be very happy here.

I could picture where to build the barn, how the lush green fields would look when they were cleared. In my mind something was taking shape: an ambitious equestrian facility where I could train horses and teach people to ride. On paper, at least, the future

Singin' Saddles Ranch was forming. I was about to chase *my* dream—not someone else's. My future was with horses, and I was taking the reins. In the meantime, one thing was certain: I was buying this land.

A week later, I signed the papers transferring ownership to me. Rick had agreed as a condition of sale to fence in an area near the trailer for my horse. I moved what little furniture I could into the trailer and put the rest in storage. Angel Babe was trailered over in a two-horse bumper-pull, and led into a corral fashioned from round cedar logs. The half-acre enclosure offered a breathtaking view of hills then covered with the rich green grass of early June. Angel circled the perimeter with glee, kicking up her heels and whinnying.

December, for her part, trotted in her dignified manner ahead of me and into the trailer. Humble though it was, this was my place. No money owed, no one to answer to. Peace, I was sure, would come to me here. I smiled and looked up at the big horseshoe hung over the front door, the heels pointing up. I sat on the bed, and when December rested her head on my knee, I ruffled her fur. "It's okay, girl," I told her. "This is our new home." I fell asleep easily, my ears almost throbbing with the silence.

❈　　　❈　　　❈

As is often the case in small New England towns, word of my arrival spread quickly. The buzz in the general store was that an eligible young woman who had been severely burned and awarded a large sum of money had bought the Goodnow property, where she was living with her horse and dog. It wasn't long before I was besieged by both contractors and suitors. Excavators, well drillers, electricians, plumbers, carpenters, and builders all came around, looking for a job or a date, or both.

But with the sharks came a dolphin to the rescue. An elderly neighbor in his sixties, Dick Delano—a distant relative of Franklin Delano Roosevelt—took me under his wing and became my friend, protector, and teacher. A kind and fatherly figure, he showed me how to rototill, plant, and fertilize a garden. His wife, Ina, taught me how to can the wild blueberries and raspberries that grew in profusion on this land, and how to make jams and relishes. Dick ensured I had plenty of firewood bought and cut for the coming fall and winter. Truckloads of hardwood were dumped near the trailer, and I learned to stack and cover it and to appreciate Dick's saying about wood, how it warms you three times—on cutting, on stacking, and finally on burning.

That summer, I hired one of Dick's neighbors, a carpenter, to build a small wooden three-stall barn inside the corral. One stall would house Angel, another grain and hay, and the last one my tack and grooming equipment. As fall approached, we celebrated the new barn with a bonfire one night. Neighbors and friends feasted on a keg of beer, hot dogs, and sweet roasted corn on the cob. A few of us picked out tunes on our guitars around the flickering flames.

Even Angel Babe joined the party. Unbeknownst to us, she had figured out how to tap the keg, and several hours later was seen staggering around the new barn.

Drunk or sober, Angel was no angel, and she would have to go. All my thoughts now were devoted to creating an equestrian facility (I had even declined to renew my teaching contract to focus on my dream), and I spent every weekend going to horse shows in surrounding states—Vermont, Massachusetts, Connecticut. At a New England Paint and Pinto Horse Club show in Raymond, New Hampshire, I took note of a tall, slim fellow in his thirties, dressed meticulously in cowboy garb. With his thick, dark curly hair and good looks, Jay Mele had presence, and women fell like dominoes at a glance from him. But it was his skill as a horseman that appealed to me most. As I watched him maneuver not one but several horses through jumping, trail, and barrel-racing events, he showed what a gifted rider he was. He had a soft, contained calm with his horses. Jay never forced himself on them, but rather coaxed them into offering themselves to him.

At the end of the show, I mustered enough courage to introduce myself. President of the local paint horse club, Jay was cordial, and he gave me a soda to go with his handshake. I showed him a photo of Angel Babe and asked him if he knew of anyone who might be interested. Not long afterward, a family from Connecticut arrived at my place. They were looking for a jumper for their daughter, and it seemed that Angel had a knack for that discipline. A rider put a jumping saddle on her, worked her a bit on the flat in walk, trot, and canter and then arranged several dead trees, first into a cross-rail and then into a vertical fence. Angel sailed over the jumps effortlessly. She would finally find her niche—in the show ring (devoid of deer, cows, and trucks).

But with Angel gone, I was now once more horseless. Meanwhile, back at Mass General, doctors marveled at the progress I had made in walking and using my left hand. Though my fingers were still bent and misshapen, I could function with that hand in a normal way. No more surgeries for me. I'd had enough. The reconstruction of my body was over.

The doctors urged me to continue the therapy I had devised myself: riding my horse and playing my guitar. My hunt for a new horse began, and it occurred to me that Larry Gagnon might have something for me. Turns out he did.

I walked down the aisle at Larry's place in Avon, Connecticut, my guide the brunette I'd come to recognize. She was pointing out horses for sale. "This palomino gelding is for sale," she offered. "He'd make you a good horse."

I shook my head. "No, I don't think so. He'd only remind me of my last palomino." There would be no Bailey II in my life.

We walked past an Appaloosa, then gray, sorrel, and chestnut quarter horses, none of whom appealed. I was about to turn around to go when I spotted in the end stall a chestnut and white pinto gelding with sapphire-blue eyes. Just shy of fifteen hands, he was the most unusual horse I had ever seen, a tobiano pattern, with dark chestnut hair masking his haunting eyes. He had a long white forelock and a lovely, flowing, two-toned mane, with a tail so long it dragged the ground behind him.

(A few definitions might be in order here. A paint horse is a breed that can be registered with the American Paint Horse Association. A pinto is a spotted horse of any breed. A tobiano horse is a spotted horse with calico markings—generally white legs and some white over the back. And an overo horse is a spotted horse with no white over the back.)

"What about this horse?" I asked. "Is he for sale?"

"You mean Dial? Yeah, I think he is, but I'll have to check with the boss man."

"What do you know about him?" I probed, thinking she might offer information the owner would not.

"I think he's part Arab and part saddlebred, but I'm not sure there are any papers on him," she said. "He's pretty gentle. We used him in the sharpshooting act a couple of times, and he's real quiet. A girl who used to own him didn't pay her board, and we got him. Let me get Larry for you."

She shouted for him, telling him, "Some lady wants to know about Dial." What kind of a name for a horse is that? I thought. My mind conjured soap commercials ("Dial," a jingle of the day went, "is ready when you are"). I thought of dials on clocks and meters. Maybe this Dial was pointing to me. On the other hand, I reminded myself, I was the one who thought you couldn't go wrong with a horse named Angel.

Larry walked over to me, the bow in his legs as wide as his smile. Only riding thousands of horses could make a man that bowlegged. He tipped his straw hat and nodded a hello; clearly he did not recall our previous meeting.

"You interested in this here gelding?" he asked in that megaphone voice of his.

"Maybe," I replied. "What can you tell me about him?"

"Used to be papers on him, so I was told. He's from Arizona, a Heinz variety. Around eleven or twelve, I'd say. Perfect size for a petite [he pronouced it *pee*-tight] woman like you. He's pretty well broke, sound as a dollar, no bad habits. No, I take that back. Only bad habit of his is, he eats too much. Wanna ride him?"

"Sure."

He turned to the woman. "Saddle up Dial, will ya? In that Simco job [a kind of saddle]. There might be something in it for you." He winked at her, patting her with a lingering hand.

I turned to the object of his attention and asked if she'd mind if I haltered him myself. Not at all, she said. As I opened the stall door, the blue-eyed gelding turned from his hay and started toward me. Good sign, I thought. He likes people. I slipped on his halter and told him to "whoa" while I ran my hand down his legs to feel for any heat or blemishes. His hooves were cool, as they should be, not a blemish or scar in sight.

He stood there calmly, apparently content to be handled and touched all over. I picked the pine shavings out of his mane and patted him gently on the neck, then handed the lead line to the brunette as she walked him to the cross-ties. I watched as he walked, looking for signs of interference—one leg striking another—but found none.

I could not take my eyes off his. They were light blue, what American Indians used to call "ghost eyes" or "spirit eyes." Some horse people are spooked by such eyes in a horse. I wasn't. He was strange looking, but then, so was I. Even then, in the cross-ties, he and I had this magnetic attraction. Sometimes you feel it with horses, and sometimes you don't. With Dial, I felt instant chemistry.

Gagnon's stable hand ran her brush lightly over this horse, gathered his tail and untangled the long hairs, brushing them all till they were shiny. Finally, she picked out each of his hooves, which he patiently held up for her while she sang to some Top Forty tune on the barn radio. I admired Dial's straight legs and his long sloping shoulders and pasterns, which promised a comfortable ride. His chiseled features, shining coat, and weight spoke of the good care he was receiving. If he had faults—he was overweight, and his shoes badly needed to be reset—they were easily corrected. The woman tacked him up in a black saddle with white buckstitching and led him to a small indoor arena, where I was handed the reins.

I mounted up. Dial stood quietly for this rider he had never met, not moving an inch. I warmed him up slowly in the ring and within ten minutes was pulling a rocking-horse lope out of him. My heart started to beat hard, the excitement of riding this well-trained horse bubbling up inside me. He was so responsive, much more so than Bailey. Riding Dial, you thought something and he did it. It was like moving from a car with manual steering to one with power steering.

I walked him outside the arena to see how he'd respond to things that scare some horses—tall wet grass blowing in the breeze, grain bags, tractors and trailers—and then I brought him close to the road when a large dump truck whizzed past. Dial never flinched.

Larry called out, "So, whaddya think of him? Isn't he just like I told you?"

Not wanting to sound overeager, I replied, "Well, I really planned on buying a younger horse, more of a challenge."

The old horse trader countered. "In your condition, darlin', you want a horse like Dial here. He'll never rear up on you or spook, even if you light a string of firecrackers underneath him. You can ride him all day, right in traffic. Real dependable. He's the best-looking paint I've ever seen."

In my condition. I ignored that gaffe and the other one (this horseman clearly didn't know the difference between a paint and a pinto, which Dial was).

"So how much are you asking for him?" I wanted to know.

"Not enough," he smirked. "Twenty-five hundred dollars for you, cash money. For anyone else, maybe more."

"Has he ever been lame or colicked?" I asked.

"Nope," came the reply. "Never had that laminitis [though it came out *lame*initis]. No cowlicks either [he meant colic]." I grinned at his fracturing of the language, chalking it up to poor hearing and limited education. Meanwhile, leaning toward a purchase, I launched my final question.

"Any holes in this horse, Mr. Gagnon?" I wanted to spare myself any surprises if I took the horse home to Westmoreland, and I trusted Larry Gagnon to admit to them.

"Only hole will be in your pocketbook," he said. "Nope, this horse is as honest as they come." I unsaddled him and led him back to his stall. Leaning over the door, Dial nuzzled me and rested his head on my shoulder, as if daring me not to buy him.

"All right, it's a deal," I told Larry. "But only if you trailer him to my place in New Hampshire."

"Deal," the trader said.

That night, as I lay in bed, I was picturing myself in full western dress sitting in a fine saddle atop that blue-eyed horse. I couldn't sleep. There was such hope, such a promise of light, in this kind and trusting horse. I had no idea then how important Dial would become, how smart he really was, how our partnership would shape the course of my life. Dial the Trickster, they would call him. He would be my stage partner for seventeen years.

12

Blue-eyed Horse,
Blue-eyed Man

WE WERE INSEPARABLE, Dial and I. Running in his paddock, whinnying and spraying dirt and very much full of himself, my chestnut
pinto looked and acted like a graceful yearling. His muscle tone
improved with active duty. Every day he would carry me over mountain paths, across rushing streams, over fallen logs and all around
town. It didn't matter if we passed renegade cattle, if deer bounded
in front of us, or if noisy garbage trucks rattled by us. Dial seemed to
take pride in protecting me, his scarred and still weak-in-the-legs
rider. He was a smooth steady mount who slowed on tight turns and
took small precise steps on steep inclines. He watched both trail and
road calmly and refused to be tempted—not once—by mouthfuls of
leaves or grass. Never had I felt so safe and well-cared-for. All alone,
without the security of the herd, Dial never balked, never looked
back to the barn, whinnied, or tried to turn for home. Once, during

an unexpected thunderstorm, he carried me quickly and safely home, jumping downed trees with grace and alacrity.

Dial and I became quite the pair, riding to the post office to pick up the mail and then Pony Expressing it home, or stopping at the general store for bread and milk. Neighbors often gave him an apple or carrot, small payment for the privilege of seeing him ride by. Neighborhood children loved him, too. On roller skates or skateboards in summer and on sleds or skis in winter, they would hang on to a long rope and shout gleefully as Dial pulled them along.

Dial carried me where my own legs would not. In exchange, I cared for him as best I knew. Daily I mucked out his stall, adding fluffy pine shavings as necessary and bringing him his feed, along with the vitamins and trace elements he needed. I held him when the farrier made his rounds, and wormed him regularly. Often, I'd just lean on the fence and watch him play with gate latches and halters to amuse himself—and me as well. Dial had a single facial whorl several inches below his eyes: the sign, says trainer Linda Tellington-Jones, of an unusually imaginative and intelligent horse with an interesting character.

If we skipped a day of riding, I sat in the pasture with him. Often I'd read to him. Our conversations were long and deep. People speak of a soul mate. I had found mine—in a horse.

Countless times, Dial and I would walk the property while I continued to sketch out in my mind the locations of pastures, indoor arena, house and barn, and all the rest. Most important, Dial helped banish the melancholy and loneliness. Because I needed a clear head while working with him—he vastly outweighed me, and there was no sense giving him an advantage—I stopped taking all my prescription painkillers, sleeping pills, and antidepressants. Besides, nothing compared with the almost electrical charge of the wind whistling through my hair as Dial galloped beneath me. Except maybe a real good kiss.

One muggy September morning, I returned home after a ride with Dial and was putting away my tack when I noticed the sky stacked high with thunderheads reaching over the mountains. The blackening clouds soon made good on their promise. After a low rumble of thunder, the air suddenly turned cooler, and with that came the first wave of that fresh familiar damp smell, of rain on earth.

I stood in Dial's stall while the rain gushed down from every corner of the roof and drummed on the metal above me. Dial stood near me, curious about my lunch—a roast beef sandwich. He sniffed at it, then curled up his lip at the pungent odor of horse-radish, as horses do when they smell something strong. I laughed at his funny face and held it under his nostrils again, wanting to provoke the same response, which it did.

It looks, I thought, as though he's smiling when he curls his lip like that. It took me back to the time I had taught Bailey how to hug me and give me a kiss. I had just seen Larry Gagnon in the show ring with his trick horse and I must have been eager to master a few tricks of my own back at Mar-Bel's. I had, I told myself, taught December to fetch and retrieve, to catch a ball, to beg and crawl, and I had taught my parrot a few entertaining tricks. How much different could it be with a horse? It would take time, of which I had plenty, and patience. I thought it would be good for Bailey. He had basic education; what he needed then was something to stimulate his mind—call it charm school. The reward for me would be communication with my horse on a finer and higher level.

I remember leaning over the fence, showing Bailey a carrot to pique his interest, and then placing the carrot by my cheek. "C'mon, fella," I urged him while making a smacking noise with my lips. "Give me a kiss." As he reached for the orange tidbit, Bailey's big lips brushed my cheek.

I was exuberant. I fed him the carrot, showered him with praise, and rubbed his neck vigorously. I tried it again, and I hardly minded that he drooled carrot all over my face. Bailey was a quick study. When Melly chanced by, I bragged about Bailey giving me a kiss.

"Yeah, but it's from a horse!" he shot back.

"A kiss is still a kiss," I replied. "And a rose by any other name would smell as sweet."

Perhaps so, Melly conceded, then added as he turned to leave, "At least he won't kiss and tell."

But if Bailey was quick off the mark, Dial was quicker. That day in New Hampshire, as the downpour continued, I fumbled in my pocket for some carrots, and held the sandwich up to Dial again, this time adding the oral command, "Smile!" When he did, he got the carrot. After a few times, he caught on, and it wasn't long before simply approaching his muzzle with my finger provoked the smile and the paycheck—one carrot—that came with it. Eventually, no carrots as rewards. Just praise.

Dial's repertoire, and mine, would grow. It was the beginning of a beautiful relationship.

Dial, it turns out, was a ham. When friends came to visit or we encountered neighbors during rides, I couldn't resist showing them what he had learned. Nor could Dial resist putting on a show. He would curl his lips in a smile and endear himself to all who saw him.

As his vocabulary of tricks grew, he would trot them out at random in pursuit of a carrot treat. Onlookers thought him a veritable four-legged genius, a wonder horse. He wasn't just yearning for the carrot; he was reacting to my joy, for my whole face lit up when he performed. I would get so excited, literally jump up and down and clap my hands and tell him how wonderful and brilliant he was. Horses, like most domesticated animals, understand and appreciate praise. If I had no carrots, I would reward Dial for a trick—whether asked for or offered unbidden—by rubbing and scratching his favorite spot by his withers. He would lean into that rub and make that face, his "It feels soooooooooooo good" face.

I began to study Dial carefully to see what other natural responses of his I could mold into tricks. I watched, for example, as he shook off flies and tried to bite at them, or pawed the ground when he was impatient. I was learning how to think like a horse, to read his mind by reading his body. I thought, if I can imitate a fly, I could teach Dial to shake his head as if he were saying "Yes" and "No." By tapping his leg with a long dressage whip and imitating the touch of a fly, perhaps he would paw and appear to be counting. And my reasoning worked. By lightly—ever so lightly—pricking his neck and chest with a nail file, I taught him to nod and shake his head, offering a carrot for every try, until his response became routine. Meanwhile, Dial was teaching me a great deal. To quote the grand old man of horse trainers, Tom Dorrance ("the horse's lawyer"), "What I know I learned from the horse."

I have worked with so many trick horses since, but Dial was the first, and he laid down the foundation. With each successive horse, I learned more about the art of trick-horse training. I could see each horse learning, could almost see the lightbulbs going off in their brains. The whole process became so addictive, so much fun.

As a trick-horse trainer, my mantras—some practical, some philosophical—would become these:

When the horse gives a little, praise a lot.
Love and kindness are both the method and the reward.
What you give is what you get back.
You must be quiet to hear them speak.
Everything in sequence.
Always work the horse in the same spot. It's like his desk at school.
Always end on a good note.
Wean the horse off treats quickly.

During winters in New Hampshire before the indoor riding arena was built, riding would slow down—but not my involvement with the horses. I'd spend time rubbing and grooming, learning just how hard or soft to rub, careful to learn each horse's likes and dislikes, and hand-feeding them carrots.

At this point Gary and I had a team of workhorses, several saddle horses, and Dial. The quiet country setting offered me the company of nature, the pleasure of seeing deer, fox, and wild turkeys. Peace came to me from watching the horses munching contentedly, protected from the cold in their blankets and in clean, freshly bedded stalls. I traded in my long skirts and sandals for Levi's, sweatshirts, and work boots. My closets now contained flannel shirts, down jackets, Sorel insulated boots, yellow hooded and heavy raincoats, pebbly gloves and fleece ear warmers.

And I couldn't live without my cherished tools: the manure fork and wheelbarrow. I used the latter to haul hay bales—forty-pound bales stacked to the rafters—as well as shavings, sand, firewood, and manure. Though my body ached at first, it soon became capable and strong.

The stalls—free of distractions, so the horse would have to pay attention to me—were ideal for teaching tricks. I'd make Dial use his fine mind by asking him to listen to my cues and pick up a hat, or discriminate and pick one object but not another, to count and bow in the soft shavings. I loved the confidence and trust he gave me. Dial knew my voice. He even knew the sound of my truck and would whinny when he heard it.

But in the early 1980s, as the finishing touches were being put on Singin' Saddles Ranch, I had a lot to learn about teaching horses tricks, and there was little literature available to help me. There were, I knew, trick-horse trainers in circuses and in Hollywood, but they were distant resources. My thoughts turned to the big cocky man down the road who had sold me Dial—Larry Gagnon.

"So, you come here to pick my brain, did you?" he snarled when I explained my mission. He still had a knack for intimidation. "If I tell you how to do this, then I'll be out of work!"

"I thought . . . ," I stammered.

"You thought what? That I'd show you what it took me fifteen years to learn the hard way?"

Larry's wife, Lucy, a slender and attractive woman with olive skin—a woman I would later grow close to and admire—spoke up on my behalf.

"Larry, it won't hurt to show her something. After all, she bought Dial from you. I don't think she's going to be stealing any bread from your table." She winked at me. I nodded, grateful for her intervention.

Larry shrugged. "All right, then. But just watch and don't be asking me any questions."

I'll be as quiet as a mouse, I thought. Mighty Mouse.

And so began weekly hikes for several months to Larry's place at Avon. I watched him carefully as he put Black Diamond, his black Thoroughbred stud, and his leopard Apppy, Domino, through their routines. Never once did I dare ask how he trained the handsome stallion to stretch, bow, kneel, lie down, rear, or pose on a pedestal. Sheepishly, I nodded in agreement when he spoke to me, just glad of the opportunity to see a trick-horse trainer work. Repeatedly, Larry had me cue the stallion to do tricks. Out in the ring, Larry hollered at me, "Look up at the audience, not at the horse! Be confident! Smile, for chrissakes! Sit up straight and act proud! Watch where you point that whip. He's watching every move you make. Tap him like you mean it, not like some sort of wimp!"

On this point, Larry Gagnon and I would differ profoundly. Though one could not argue with his results, his methods left much to be desired. He was as intimidating with horses as he was with people, and though he put out a pamphlet calling for trainers to use gentleness, he seemed to possess little of it himself. I was grateful that this trick-horse trainer had shown me a few things, but I lamented that the threat of punishment—and not just the chance of reward—figured so prominently in his thinking. I was sure I could do with kindness what he accomplished with force.

I learned to take what Larry said with a grain of salt. I let slide his jibes about my riding and my techniques, and I tried not to laugh when Larry put his foot in his mouth. I once looked on as he bragged in the company of Glen Randall that he, Larry, had trained Trigger, the legendary palomino ridden by Roy Rogers. Glen stepped forward, saying he wanted to shake the hand of the man who had trained Trigger—but the joke was all on Larry. I knew, as did many there, that Glen had trained Trigger. Larry ate crow that night, though he tried to cover by insisting that one of Trigger's stand-ins had stayed overnight at his farm.

Dial taught me far more than Larry ever did, though I would always remain grateful that he had sold me my blue-eyed beauty. My horse taught me to break down each trick into bite-sized pieces. The curtsy bow, for example, really begins with teaching the horse to stretch, which in turn requires that the horse understand every step of the process. He has to learn to hold his head above his back, and to keep it there. He then has to learn to stretch out all four feet, first the front ones, then the rear, and, again, to hold that pose. Muscles in the horse's back need to be developed slowly for the stretch.

The curtsy bow builds from there. You simply induce the horse, while in a stretch, to draw his head down low between his legs—at first in quest of a piece of carrot, and later on verbal command and whip cues. When the whole thing is put together and the horse pulls off his bow in a matter of seconds, it looks smooth and easy. But many days and weeks have gone into that one trick. Once it is taught on the ground and is solid, teaching the same trick from the saddle is another process.

The trainer has to learn where to place his or her hands, where to be looking, where and how to tap with the dressage whip (used as an extension of the hand), how to offer a small carrot piece while looking away and without losing a finger to the horse's teeth. The trainer has to learn how to ignore unwanted responses, prevent evasions, reward desired behavior immediately, and over time, wean the horse off treats so the horse doesn't become a "food junkie." The treat is merely a motivator, an instant "paycheck." What you want is a horse working for praise, or better, working simply because he loves to work.

Vicki Hearne, the late Connecticut horsewoman, author, and animal trainer, argued—persuasively, I think—that the happy horse is one who knows his job and takes satisfaction from doing it well. In *Animal Happiness*, she wrote, "My thinking, such as it is, I learned from the animals, for whom happiness is usually a matter of getting the job done. Clear that fence, fetch in those sheep, move those calves, win that race, find that guy, retrieve that bird." The trick horse is no different: job satisfaction is everything.

Most of this wisdom I learned by trial and error, with the help of many many sacks of carrots. Dial always tried hard for me, despite my lack of method in the beginning. What mattered most to me was the close partnership we enjoyed. We were both getting to know the other's personality, and he seemed to find joy in my joy, and to try hard to figure out what provoked it.

Each new trick he learned inspired me to learn another one. Soon Dial was stretching, bowing, kneeling, lying down, and sitting up, and it wasn't long before he had thirty tricks in his repertoire. I blissfully—and, as I look back on it, mindlessly—dreamed about sharing his talent with a wider audience. Soon I would learn that limelight in a dream is one thing; actual limelight quite another.

Yet I had much to be thankful for. A blue-eyed horse had changed my life, but so would a blue-eyed man.

Music was my bridge to Gary Arthur Fletcher. Gary's brother Phil and his wife, Wilma, lived just down the road from my place in Westmoreland. I had been taking weekly private guitar lessons at a music store in Brattleboro, but I yearned for the fun of jamming with fellow musicians. And I knew that Phil had played professionally in a bluegrass band—with the Berkshire Mountain Boys— and that he had toured the East Coast and even played on the radio in Nashville. Overcoming my fear of rejection, I went over to Phil's place one night and introduced myself. I got the "Howdy, neighbor!" welcome. Wilma invited me to dinner, and Phil showed me his impressive collection of records, tapes, and vintage instruments: guitars, banjos, violins. Phil, I learned, played a 1952 D28 Martin guitar. His brother Pete played a 1959 D18 Martin. I loved down-home, knee-slappin', toe-tappin' music, and getting hooked on it was easy.

The Fletcher tribe—a family of ten siblings—were well known around the homestead in Keene, New Hampshire. Family get-togethers invariably meant laughter and food and live music, old-time country music from the 1930s, '40s and '50s—songs like "Walkin' the Floor over You" and "Cattle Call." Phil had a fine voice, much like Gene Autry's, and he showed me how to pick the guitar to bluegrass and country tunes. We practiced a few times a week, harmonizing our voices, even yodeling in harmony on hundreds of songs.

But Phil, it seems, was not just a music maker; he was a match-maker as well. At the very least, he was looking out for his younger brother and trying to send some work his way. One evening, I told Phil of my plans for an equestrian facility on my property. What you need, he replied, is a good logger/carpenter/builder. You need, in other words, my little brother Gary.

Phil then sang Gary's praises. Gary had built numerous roads; he had, in fact, cut in the road to the trailer I now called home. He had also constructed many log homes, had built his parents' house and worked on those of four of his brothers, including Phil's. Gary had a reputation for helping others, and people flocked to him to get things fixed (thus his nicknames—Gizmo, Gizzy, Giz), to have him adjust the sights on their guns, for help or advice on some project. The résumé sounded impressive, and I agreed to meet Gary for dinner.

In fact, I had previously met Gary Fletcher with one of his brothers in a bar-restaurant called Henry David's (as in Thoreau) in Keene. Ironically, this was the same place I had chosen to bid a less than fond farewell to Scott several months beforehand. I had purposefully chosen a public place to reduce the risk of a scene and had insisted we meet there, so each of us could retreat in our own cars. It was a teary and tempestuous parting, with me accusing him of angling for my bank account (which he denied) and him dismissing my plans for a horse operation as just so much false hope.

I look back on that time and have to believe that were it not for my dream—a life with horses and a grand facility to launch that life—my fate could have taken a sinister turn. I was still badly depressed from the fire, still going back and forth to Mass General for all those surgeries, still in pain and entitled to painkillers. I was living in a trailer, alone, and taking pills to sleep at night. In the evenings, I would often go to bars and contra dances—a kind of free-form square dancing to banjo and piano—and put back beer, wine, mixed drinks. Anything to forget.

For the first time in my life, I was using pills and booze to drown my sorrows. The loneliness and self-doubt, the falling out with Scott and the fear that no man would love me for the person I was, all drove me to overindulge after dark. Looking back on it, I trust an instinct telling me that this behavior was likely temporary, and even understandable under the circumstances.

Still, I wonder. Had it not been for the responsibility of taking care of my animals and the need to keep a clear head while working with them, would I have abandoned these poisons? Perhaps not. My animals, though, needed me. They had to be fed twice daily, watered, groomed, cleaned, and exercised. And I wasn't going to let them down, for they trusted me.

And while Gary Fletcher was, and remains, a gifted builder, he too had demons that he sought to drown in alcohol. With his full beard and shock of blond hair, his savvy in the woods, his skill with a hunting rifle and a fishing rod, he reminded me then of a woodsy movie character of the day called Jeremiah Johnson—a mountain man who survives in the Rocky Mountain wilderness. But where Johnson was a strapping big man, Gary was diminutive and sinewy.

He was always lean, a little hungry-looking. When I first met him, he would make jokes about the poverty he knew as a boy. How cardboard would be deployed to squeeze a few more months out of an old pair of shoes, how the Salvation Army dropped off a food basket some Christmases. The only meat they had at home was what they hunted: deer, moose, bear, wild turkey, duck, pheasant. There was too little money to adequately feed and clothe that tribe of twelve, and what money there was, the old man drank away.

Living on the edge of absolute poverty, with a worn-ragged mother and an abusive father, made one truth apparent to Gary and his siblings: keep your mouth shut, and get out of the house as soon as you can. In a way, Gary was lucky. He was considered by many of his siblings to be favored by his father. Gary was singled out for work. On Friday nights, while his brothers were off playing their guitars and honing the musical talent that would bring some light and joy to Fletcher family gatherings, Gary was in his father's basement. One of Pop Fletcher's sidelines was tuning and sharpening chain saws, and at this Gary would show a great talent.

It seemed a short hop from there to logging, road building, carpentry, and house building, with its attendant branches—electrical work, plumbing, drywalling, roofing—not to mention his other talents as cabinetmaker, welder, mechanic, and big equipment operator. The old man had taught young Gary a few skills and instilled in him an unshakable work ethic. But he also left a terrible legacy.

With every sip of Pickwick Ale, with every flogging or stinging slap, the Fletcher children must have walked the thinnest line between love and hate, sanity and madness, life and death. The old man was a tyrant who vented his hatred on others at every chance. The code at 98 Park Avenue was this: you never broke the silence. What was broken was your will, as you were deprived of your voice, your joy, your anger, your sadness.

For young Gary, work was an escape from this humiliation and the prison of his childhood. At twelve, he had a paper route; he weeded cornfields and took on countless other jobs. Away from home was always better than at home. As is true of many of his siblings, his childhood traumas left mental barriers, an inner void and an emotional blandness that prodded him to harm himself with alcohol.

So consider the tandem that was now forming in the hills of Westmoreland in the late 1970s. Carole and Gary, two burnt-out cases. We had come to our present states from different directions, me from privilege, him from poverty. But on one matter we agreed. Each of us had reason, or so we thought, to drink. And we did. Until we found new direction, through work—though not right away.

I was skeptical at first. Before I employed Gary, I wanted to see places he had cleared and homes he had built. Off we went in Gary's rickety old truck, the bed filled with chain saws, tire chains, and peaveys (long hooked tools used to lever logs into place). Gary showed me roads cut through the forest and log houses tucked neatly away in the hills. He showed me the many kinds of trees the land around there had to offer. Though I knew nothing about construction and he knew everything, Gary was always respectful, deferential, never condescending.

He struck me as kind and honest, shy and cheerful, with a sense of humor much like my father's. When we first met in that bar, he said to me, "My name is Gary. How do you like me so far?" In his New Hampshire lilt, *far* came out *fawh,* and *yards* came out *yahds,* as in "the whole nine yahds," one of his favorite expressions. He had others: "just like pea soup" meant good, very good; "hot enough to breed sheep" was hot, very hot; "faster than a rooster on a june bug" was indeed fast; and when something broke, it "shit the bed." There was about him, always, the smell of pine, and there were pitch stains on his jeans. I liked him right off the bat, and better yet, I trusted him.

"So, how would you start clearing my land?" I asked him.

"Well, there are two ways you can do it," he said. "With a log skidder, or with horses. A skidder will make a mess in the woods, taking down all small trees in its path. It might be faster, but it sure is messier."

My thoughts drifted back to the pioneers who used horses to clear land, to plow, plant, and till. I went to see George Edwards, a local celebrity at horse pullings and fairs. After showing me his prized old farm equipment, harrows, antique snow rollers, and a room full of harness-making and leather-working tools, he introduced me to his seventeen-hand, two-thousand-pound Percheron draft horse, Jim.

On the spot I contracted this man and his horse. George and

Jim would pull out the trees that Gary cut down and drag them to a portable sawmill to be cut up for lumber. That huge horse worked tirelessly, from morning to late afternoon. Attentive to even subtle commands from George, Jim would move oaks and pines thirty to forty feet long and weighing two to three tons. The huge oaks would become the timbers for the new post-and-beam house that was taking shape in my mind.

By now I was reading *Mother Earth News,* and books on homesteading and raising livestock. I was learning how to bake and cook, make jams and jellies. My quest was to become physically independent and self-sufficient. As I grew stronger, I became convinced that the physical stamina required to live in the country—lifting and stacking hay bales, stacking wood—would make me stronger still. The rural life, the simpler life, suited me.

Gary would make sketches and show them to me. This was my dream, and he was my hired hand, but our relationship tilted early on toward partnership—a business partnership, I thought. I was impressed with his craftsmanship, his precision (later I would tease him that he even cut cheddar cheese using a carpenter's level). His motto—and I was appreciating it more and more—was an old one: No job is worth doing if you don't do it well.

And though he teased me about my passion for antiques and anything old, he understood it and even humored me. One time I told him that I admired the big forged hinges once commonly used on old doors. No problem, he said. He fired up some wood in an old metal barrel and forged me some hinges. I had the feeling there was nothing he could not do.

Meanwhile, it seemed that Lady Luck was also with our project.

One day, while I was out riding Dial, a man approached me and asked if I'd be interested in buying a team of well-broke, matched Belgian draft horses, a half brother and sister. I knew the pair of sorrels he was referring to, Scythe and Sickle, and jumped at the chance to own my own team. The horses were sound and service-able, and we used them to clear the remaining land. When all the fields had been cleared of trees, the stumps removed, and the soil harrowed and seeded, I had twenty-five acres ready to accommo-date house, barns, and pastures. Along the way I had spent many days behind those Belgians with the sun shining and the birds singing, pleasures I would have been denied were I sitting in the enclosed cab of a skidder with headphones on.

New England is known for its rocks (New Hampshire is the Granite State), and the land at Westmoreland had more than its share. Gary and I enlisted the aid of Boy and Girl Scout troops, col-lege and church clubs, to help us clear the fields of rocks. In exchange for their labor, we'd hitch up the team and give them hay rides. And when that work was done, we continued to offer hay rides in summer and sleigh rides in winter—both on my property and at local events—to generate income.

During all this time, my working relationship with Gary became more of a friendship. When we weren't planning roads, wells, septic fields, house, and barns, and making the myriad deci-sions that mark such projects, this blue-eyed woodsman was taking me to auctions and on fishing trips. On weekends, he would look on as I practiced with Phil, murmuring every word of the bluegrass and country songs he'd grown up with.

An "easy keeper," in horse parlance, is a steady, undemanding horse who does his job well, keeps his weight, and causes no worries to his owner. Gary was like that. Were he a particular breed of horse, I would have said he was an all-purpose Morgan—steady and quiet, talented but humble, and easy to be with. He was helping to banish some of the loneliness that had crept up on me.

And because he was so at home in the woods and in the countryside, he helped me feel comfortable there too. A true outdoorsman, he well knew the habits of wildlife—where the deer bedded down and made their scrapes, what food was available to them. He was in terrific shape, both from his work and from tracking down deer in the woods, up and down ledges, and then dragging them out. When he got a trophy buck (like a two-hundred-pound deer with an eight-point rack, whose stuffed head now hangs in our living room in Florida), he got it by hunting and tracking, not by sitting in a tree. When he fished, he caught his own bait first and sought out the fish. And always, he hunted and fished not for sport but to put food on the table.

With friends, he once drove all the way to Wyoming in a truck pulling a horse trailer, which housed a huge freezer powered by a gas generator. Gary and his pals hunted deer and antelope for a week, filled the freezer with venison, and then drove back to New Hampshire.

I could not believe how strong he was for his height and weight. There wasn't an ounce of fat on him, with his Popeye arms and muscles from carrying around a twenty-eight-pound Jonsered chain saw in the forest. He would pile huge long logs on a skidway by himself. "I use my thinking equipment first," he'd say. Brain before brawn.

Gary and I started dating informally, joining others at bluegrass concerts or going to equipment and antiques auctions. One time he took me ice fishing on Lack Champlain—a first for me. I was all bundled up, and he was dressed in a light hunting jacket, woolen hunting pants, and toque. We drove out onto the ice in his truck, and I watched him work the hand auger in his bare, weathered hands. Through sixteen inches of solid ice he drilled—fifteen holes, fifteen seconds each. Then he set up the ice tip-ups and baited the hooks. The guy in the fishing hut next to us could hardly believe how quickly the job was done. Gary was a man on a mission, and if he was trying to impress me, it worked. This was one salty guy.

I got to know his appetites. He loved meat and potatoes and gravy, and homemade apple pie like his mother used to make. He ate peanut butter on everything but could not abide those stalwarts of his childhood, chipped beef on toast or oatmeal. He smoked Marlboro cigarettes and drank Miller beer; later it was coffee or Pepsi. He saved everything (lumber, copper tubing, old tools), convinced he'd find a use for them, and usually he did. And after every job, especially dirty jobs, he relied on waterless hand cleaner to take the grit away.

The more I got to know him, the more I realized how soft and gentle he was. Gary would tease me, and I loved to be teased, though I had never mastered the art myself. I had grown up virtually an only child and never got to practice the cut-and-thrust that individuals in large families learn as a survival mechanism. Gary would tease me about always being cold (with his Popeye arms, he called himself the "arm strong heater"), or my preference for old things over new—like the old wooden pull-chain toilet I had him install, against his advice, and which later leaked like a sieve.

What I came to admire in Gary was how he learned to triumph over his past. By talking about his childhood wounds, he was able to free up his emotions. He came to accept and even forgive his past, and to live in the present. And so did I.

Our romance was slow and gradual, not like so many of my other courtships, which had been of the head-over-heels type and thus doomed to failure. Several years went by, and we ended up living in the trailer while the house was being built. Still, we never committed to each other, for we were both gun-shy. Gary kept seeing his brothers divorce, and I had been down that path twice.

And there was the drinking. Eventually we did seal our partnership, but only after I had quit my own ruinous behavior. The routine and responsibility of looking after horses helped instill healthier habits. And the satisfaction I gained from training horses allowed me to shake hands with my grief and to part company. I invited Gary to do likewise. "I love you very much," I told him, "but I cannot live with an alcoholic." That was nineteen years ago.

In all that time, he has never wavered. Nor has he ever wavered in his support for what I do. Even in exasperating times, he has backed me. A friend of mine once observed that while I had, in essence, married my father when I married Gary, Gary had essentially married his mother. There's some truth in that.

Like my father, Gary was a hunter who adored animals. In fact, Gary's love for animals rivals my own. He has had dogs his whole life—foremost a beloved black Lab retriever called Blue. Another, a yellow Lab, arrived as a pup at a logging camp all covered in pine pitch, thus Gary's name for him, Pitch. One time, after a farmer had told Gary that four orphaned week-old raccoon pups were huddled in a tree, he rescued them all. He gave three away and kept the fourth, the smallest male, which he called Benny, as a pet for thirteen years. Gary had a red-tailed hawk he called Big Red, and spent two years nurturing the raptor back to health from a broken wing; Gary would capture pigeons under the bridge in Brattleboro as food for him. Even now, anyone who shows a kindness to our dogs Fancy and Dewey is showing a kindness to Gary; he delights in seeing them doted upon, especially young Fancy, for whom he has a soft spot.

At our place in New Hampshire, Gary raised our own cows and pigs, and he'd often bring one or two of the weaker piglets into the house to keep them warm. He had boars with names such as Homer S. Bradley (the name of a local lawyer), Ulysses S. Grunt, and Luigi (named after an Italian neighbor), and a huge old sow (eight hundred pounds) named Molly.

And, like my father, though quieter by nature, Gary is also a nurturer of humans as well as animals. He may be uncomfortable expressing affection—certainly in public—but he shows his love for me and my horses by all that he has built, and by building with care. Every stall, every barn, every cherry staircase or maple floor, all the gifts he has made for me (a tack tote of dovetailed cherry-wood, a tack trunk of honeyed pine, a horseshoe lamp, horseshoe saddle stands), are like enduring Valentines.

Finally, like my father, Gary loves a good joke and prizes wit. When Gary finds something funny, truly funny, he almost collapses with laughter, bent at the waist, eyes closed, mouth open. He is a small man with a big laugh, a contagious laugh that sets all around him laughing too.

Gary's mother was a saint; at least he saw her that way. He remembers her rising in the middle of the night to bake bread for the family in a wood cookstove, washing endless diapers on a washboard, sewing clothes but never buying herself a new dress. He remembers all the sacrifices she made, and how, by sheer willpower, she kept the Fletcher tribe together. He saw her as a pillar of strength, and told me he saw the same quality in me.

Since the day we met, everything Gary has built has been a labor of love. The huge hand-carved sign at the driveway proclaiming "Singin' Saddles Ranch," for example, set the tone for that place in New Hampshire. The house was custom-built of timber-framed red oak, and accented with stone and brick. The oak and maple plank flooring came—as did all the wood—from trees on the property. Every touch had been carefully thought out: the enclosed solar deck that offered a commanding view of the hills beyond, the stone fireplace framed in oak and deploying stone from the land's stone walls, the stained-glass windows created by local artisans, the walnut and cherry spiral staircase. The pond. The carriage barn and workshop. The big ranch hall. The equine complex with its twenty-eight stalls and indoor riding arena (where, etched into the concrete aisle entrance, were the words, "This building is dedicated to the love of horses)".

All had been years in the making, and Gary had done just about everything himself, or with help. He had even hand-forged the hinges for the windows in the barn. When the cupola and weather vane were in place, the barn was done, and it was time to celebrate.

Phil Fletcher organized enough musicians to have a band playing continuously through the night. Anyone who had worked on the buildings, their families, friends, and townspeople were all invited, as Singin' Saddles Ranch was christened a complete equestrian facility. It was the summer of 1980. In the ranch hall we set out a long table covered with a red checkered tablecloth and laden with glazed ham, turkey, and dishes of beans, corn, and coleslaw, with large tubs of beer on ice. People strolled through the barn, patting the horses, who hung their heads out the half-doors. Revellers ate, clapped to the music, or danced. The clamor of the music was so loud, I had to strain to hear myself think.

Gary took my hand and led me over to the fire, where we watched the crackling flames and the curl of gray smoke. I was acutely aware of his eyes on me and the intensity of the moment, for we were now removed from the party. Sensing an awkwardness, I diffused the silence and commented, "You look so nice, all dressed up."

"So do you," he replied. Then, raising his soda as if to toast, he added, "Congratulations on your new barn."

"Without you, Gary, it wouldn't be built. Thanks."

We clinked cans and took a sip. He put his hands on my shoulder, looked deep in my eyes, and said, "I've never met anyone with a soul as beautiful as yours. I've fallen in love with you, Carole."

He covered my mouth with his, kissing me gently. We clung to each other as if the world did not exist. A tear trickled down my face. In these mountains I had found comfort and hope, and a man who saw deep into me for what I was. That night the sky shimmered with stars, stars that had never seemed so clear and bright.

I will never forget the first time we made love and how distressed I was to be giving my fire-ravaged body to someone I cherished. It was like offering damaged goods, and he was so lean and fit and strong. "All I see," he told me that night, "is a face of courage. The face of a strong woman."

13

Out of the Shadows, into the Limelight

THE STALLS THAT Gary built soon filled up with horses. At Singin'
Saddles, horses came and went. I never tallied their number, but
I've likely owned a couple hundred horses. I've lost count of the
times I've fallen from horses, but I do remember two concussions
and a broken leg, broken fingers and toes. We had boarding horses,
lesson horses, show horses, brood mares and stallions, and early in
the spring, the foals—what horse people call "babies."

In the twenty years I spent at our place near Westmoreland, I
must have gentled fifty or sixty horses, always starting when they
were just days old, continuing while they were fillies and colts,
then yearlings and two-year-olds and into the years that followed. I
had come to my method of working with very young horses by
watching both good and bad trainers—though I saw more of the
latter. From them I learned what *not* to do. On the other hand, I

would see a happy, well-trained horse, and I would ask what got him there.

My mentor all this time was Jay Mele. He was, you will recall, president of the local paint horse club, and he had helped me sell my horse Angel Babe. He was fit and strong, and I would tease him that he was a dead ringer for Alex Trebek, the host of a game show called *Jeopardy!*. A Vietnam veteran and a recovered alcoholic who had spent years training cattle horses in Alberta, he was like me in one respect: horses had healed him as well.

During lessons at his farm in Massachusetts, Jay had taught me how to use my legs, seat, and hands. He had given me polish, made a rider out of me, preparing me for competitions at paint horse shows. Out in the ring, Jay would stand in the center, advising me calmly, always encouraging and praising my efforts, while I made mistakes on his forgiving reining and cow horses, all paints and quarter horses. He was a patient man with both people and horses, and he brought young horses along much as I did—patiently, gently, slowly. As Molière said, "The trees that are slow to grow bear the best fruit." I would say to would-be horse buyers who balked at the price of a well-trained horse, "You can pay me now, or you can pay me later."

* * *

But good training eats time. The slow, patient method gets you further ahead, but it does swallow the hours and days, the weeks and months. And asking all this of a young horse is like asking a child—who only wants to run full tilt—to tiptoe. They don't want to do that.

The "made horse" is a well-trained horse, but a lot of people don't realize all that goes into the making of one. We live in an instant world; we have fast food, microwave ovens, high-speed computers. Horses aren't like that. You have to introduce things to them slowly. People too often overwhelm a horse.

William Cavendish, a noted horse trainer of the eighteenth century, put it well. "A boy," he wrote, "is a long time before he knows his alphabet, longer before he has learned to spell, and perhaps several years before he can read distinctly; and yet, there are some people who, as soon as they get on a young horse, entirely undressed and untaught, fancy that by beating and spurring, they will make him a dressed horse in one morning only. I would fain ask such stupid people whether by beating a boy they would teach him to read without first showing him the alphabet? Sure, they would beat him to death, before they would make him read."

In the years to come, a lot of horses would teach me those training maxims, but none more so than Dial the Trickster.

Unable to contain my excitement over Dial in those early days of training, I invited Jay Mele to come and see him. Jay watched, smiling and rubbing his chin, as I put Dial through his routine.

"So," he asked me, "when are you and Dial available to give a show?" And before I could answer, he informed me that the next paint show was the following month at his place and that he would buy me dinner after the show.

"How 'bout it?"

I swallowed hard. "But—"

"No buts, Carole. I won't take no for an answer. You have a talented horse there. And he's got spots! I'm going to advertise in our newsletter that you'll be the evening's entertainment. You'll be billed as Carole and Dial the Trickster."

But buts there were. But what about my scars? But how could I perform in front of so many people without feeling self-conscious? Panic started to rise within me.

Later, I confided my doubts to Gary. He was putting on the rough-sawn siding to the new barn. In his hand was a circular saw, and he set it down, the sun full in his face. "What am I going to do, Gary? How am I going to get out there in front of all those people and perform with Dial, looking the way I do?" I was trembling. The mere thought of it made my stomach knot. It's not that I wasn't accustomed to being in front of people. Piano recitals, horse shows, choirs, plays, and teaching had all prepared me; but that was before disfigurement.

He held my face in his hands. "The audience will be watching Dial, not you," he assured me. "The focus will be on how smart your horse is."

Tears started streaming down my cheeks. I nestled in the shelter of his arms as sobs shook my whole body.

"I can't," I said.

"Can't," he said calmly and tenderly, "has never been a word in your vocabulary." He held me back a little and looked directly into my eyes. "When I look at you, Carole, I don't see any scars. I see a courageous and beautiful woman." He gently wiped away my tears with his hand, then took my hands in his. "Now, go and rehearse with that spotted horse of yours. He'll have everyone clapping for more, I assure you." I nodded and went back to my horse. Gary went back to his circular saw.

* * *

We rehearsed and rehearsed, Dial the Trickster and me. I was determined that our first performance go off without a hitch. I not only rehearsed all his tricks but integrated them into a scripted routine, which I memorized and spiced with humor. It went something like this:

Carole: "Ladies and gentlemen, I'd like to introduce you to my partner and best buddy, Dial the Trickster. Dial, are you happy to be
here today?"

(Dial nods yes.)

Carole: "Well, then, how about giving everyone a big Colgate smile?"

(Dial smiles.)

Carole: "Are you getting well paid for this?"

(Dial shakes head no.)

Carole: "You know, we've got a pretty sharp audience here. And I
bet they can do math. What is the square root of sixty-four?"

(Dial counts to four.)

Carole: "Good. Now, how many days in a week?"

(Dial counts to seven.)

Carole: "Terrific, Dial. Take a bow."

(Dial curtsies.)

Carole: "Dial, would you show everyone what you do in the morn-
ings when you get up?"

(Dial stretches.)

Carole: "And what about on Sundays?"

(He kneels on two knees.)

Carole: "And after you pray, then what?"

(Dial lies down.)

Carole: "I see. It's your day of rest. And how do you get up?"

(Dial sits. I mount him in that sitting position.)

Carole: "Take another bow, Dial."

(Dial bows.)

Carole: "Dial, show everyone what it's like in New York City. What does the Statue of Liberty look like?"

(Mounts pedestal and poses.)

Carole: How about that bronze Remington statue, *The End of the Trail?"*

(Mounts pedestal on all fours.)

Carole: "And let's show everyone what we saw at Madison Square Garden. First, what did you see in the rodeo?"

(Dial bucks.)

Carole: "And at the Lipizzan show?"

(Dial sidepasses.)

Carole: "And what else?"

(He rears.)

Carole: "I know you got tired from walking a lot. Let's show everybody what you looked like."

(Dial limps. I dismount.)

Carole: "And when I got lost, how did you show me the way home?"

(Dial pushes me.)

Carole: "Okay, Dial, give me a kiss. Let's say thanks and good night
to this great audience."
(Kisses, bows, exit.)

Practice took place wherever there were loud noises and distractions—construction noise, cars and trucks coming and going,
applause from neighbors and friends who were brought in to
accustom Dial to that noise. I even bought an outdoor spotlight and
rehearsed at night to get Dial used to glare in his eyes. To give the
routine a professional look, we practiced with music from a pocket
cassette player and made plans to use a boom box for the real performance.

My homework done, I was certain that Dial was ready. On the
other hand, I worried that if I lost my cool, Dial would reflect my
tension. What I needed was a confidence-builder. I went shopping
for a show outfit and had fun doing it. I bought makeup to hide my
scars, new white chaps, a fringed blouse with fancy pearl snaps, a
cowboy hat and boots to match. Dial, as well, got new duds—a
matching saddle blanket—that complemented his natural beauty.

Showtime came, and Dial was a star. He watched me intently
for cues and performed with the ease of an old stage veteran. The
sound of applause, the whooping and hollering, proved to be a
powerful draw for both of us, compelling us to dramatize our tricks
even more. He melted their hearts. I, too, managed to perform well
under pressure, relaxing and enjoying my sidekick and the audience's appreciation of him. People swarmed around Dial after the
show, petting him and remarking on what a genius he was.

That night, Dial got hooked on performing. Anyone who has

spent time around one horse in particular soon learns, by paying attention, to read that horse. You can tell by the horse's body language, the set of his head, the softness in his eyes, the action of his ears, whether he's happy or not. And so I can say with certainty that Dial loved to perform. The louder the applause, the more he hammed it up. You could feel a surge in him before he entered a ring. He even loved the rituals that preceded performing—the hauling by trailer, the fussing and clipping, the practice. And afterward there came the throngs of people who wanted to touch "the smart horse" or have their photo taken with him. Dial was in his glory then.

And Gary had been right about the limelight: Dial had almost all of it, and that suited me fine. After shows, the adoring crowds hardly bothered with me. Their conversation was aimed directly at Dial, whose name they already knew. Little by little, my self-consciousness over my appearance faded. As well, my horse was making me feel better about myself.

Experienced horse trainers would congratulate me on my efforts toward making the world a more horse-friendly place. They praised my incredible patience and horse-reading skills. Children and adults, otherwise unfamiliar with horses and terrified of them, delighted in my well-mannered trickster. People with no time for horses looked on in wonder. Dial was opening many doors with his tricks.

Actually, this smart horse (darn that whorl on his face!) could literally open doors. Always playful with his mouth, he learned how to open the door latch of his stall and would then saunter out into the barn corridors and liberate his buddies. We had to "Dialproof" the place. Out in his paddock, we once ran a wire across a portion of the field to stop horses from grazing there. Dial leaped over the wire; when we raised the wire, he rolled under it. Finally, we ran two strands of wire, one high, one low. Dial just stared at those wires; you could almost see his brain working.

At times, he became too smart for me. On several occasions, he started limping off cue, and fooled me into thinking he was lame. Like a child who wants to get out of doing homework, Dial was trying to avoid working. I figured it out eventually, but not until my veterinarian examined him and told me there wasn't a thing wrong with him. "Too clever," was his diagnosis.

In time, I made my goals as a trainer loftier. Dial and I even learned some of the more spectacular poses and movements, adding more pizzazz to our routines. Soon we were dancing the three-step, marching, fetching letters or cards, and performing more pedestal poses on cue. These tricks and high school movements would test my patience and perseverance as a rider and trainer. But by then I understood that my success in horse training hinged on two things—communication and conditioning. As for the former, Dial was happy to accommodate my requests if he understood what it was I wanted him to do. But he also had to be physically capable of the movement: muscle and balance had to be built up slowly and gently, and the same was true of his mind. I found that short, frequent training sessions—sometimes four or five a day— kept his attention. It seemed he used the breaks to reflect on what I had taught him, for he was often sharper in the afternoon than he had been in the morning.

And if Dial was on the learning curve, so was I. By this point, I had accumulated quite a library of books on training animals and on classical circus equitation. I had also learned to be consistent in my verbal commands, hand and whip cues, and body/leg aids. My timing improved tremendously as I realized the importance of rewarding Dial during that nanosecond of time when it was most appropriate—delivering the prize almost in the same moment as he performed the trick. Reading my horse and knowing what was going through his mind made my timing even better, because I could anticipate his actions.

And, perhaps most important, Dial learned to trust me implicitly. He knew that his safety was always uppermost in my mind, and he was so forgiving of my mistakes. When I was first teaching him to rear, I would sometimes be careless with my reins, and he'd get his front feet caught in them. He'd respond instantly to my "whoa", and never panicked, staying perfectly still while I reorganized. To prevent injuries, I always used protective front leg boots when he was being taught to perform on a pedestal, bow, kneel, or lie down. Whatever equipment I used was always safe and sturdy. Gary saw to that by building pedestals and teeter-totters that would easily hold a thousand-pound horse. I was always careful to guard my own safety as well.

Before long it became known around New England that Dial the Trickster had the charm to draw a crowd. We were an act for hire. I had professionals produce photographs, flyers, and business cards. I placed ads in equine periodicals and signed on with an animal agency.

Dial and I would please hundreds of thousands of spectators at local and state fairs, special events, festivals, local and national horse shows, resorts, rodeos, theme parks, and parades. We even did several commercials—some of them nationally televised. One, for a lottery and shot in Boston, implied that a beautiful bowing horse might come your way if you bought a ticket. In another, filmed in Keene, I was dressed like Paul Revere and rode Dial at a gallop while shouting, "The British are coming! The British are coming!"

Charities and benefits were especially rewarding. Dial posed for pictures with terminally ill children at camps and foundations (such as Paul Newman's Hole in the Wall Gang Camp and the Make-a-Wish Foundation), lighting up faces as only sitting atop a horse can do. He and I taught disabled youngsters and adults how to groom, saddle, and ride. Dial's forgiving nature helped heal many others as well as me.

※　　　※　　　※

When I first moved north to New Hampshire, and I was estranged for a time from my mother. She couldn't understand why I wanted to move there, and she didn't approve of my using the settlement money to build an equestrian center, nor did she approve of Gary. My mother had yet to meet him, for he was a gentile.

My father, though, would visit me on his own. He thought the ranch was a special place, and he played endlessly with my dogs and horses. I was always glad to see him come, sad to see him go, for he never failed to lift my spirits. And he always always made me laugh.

If I am a punster, and I am, blame Irv Rosenberg. (One night recently, I took a friend to an elaborate equestrian dinner theater near

Orlando, and when a woman in the washroom later complained that the horses she petted after the show were sweaty, I advised her, "Don't pet the sweaty stuff, and don't sweat the petty stuff.")

Throughout the years of building Singin' Saddles Ranch, Dad and I had remained close. I would make solo trips, by car or train, to Florida and spend time with the family on Dad's boat. Likewise, he flew up and visited me, inspecting the building as it progressed.

Much to my surprise, my mother had convinced him to sell the boat. Too much upkeep for a man in his seventies, she told him. Without his boat, his pride and joy, he was lost. Shortly thereafter he suffered a massive stroke, one that left him paralyzed and unable to speak. A lifetime of cigarettes, steak and beer, and lobster with butter had exacted their toll.

In a coma for more than two years, he had been on life support all that time while my mother went on clinging to the doctors' small hope that he would recover. Gary and I drove down to Florida, and for the first time, my mother met Gary while we all saw my father in the hospital. I would pray for his swift death, an end to the misery.

On a day in 1986 I got the call I'd been dreading.

"We lost Dad." It was my mother on the other end, choking back tears. I felt as if I'd been hit in the head with a wrecking ball. I had prayed for his death, yet death had offered no relief. I felt only the crush of grief.

My father had been the one constant in my life, the conduit to my family during years when I was estranged from my mother. He was the man I had idolized most. He had been my confidant, my pal, he had been there when I found the land on which I had built my future. Now he was gone.

"We lost Dad." Those words undid me. Gary came over and put his arms around me, trying to console me, but there was no stopping the tears. "It's all right, Carole," he said. "He's at peace." An hour later, I was still in his arms, still sobbing.

At the funeral, I held my mother's hand during the service and burial. Both of us clung to each other, as if we knew we were all the other had left. After leaving the funeral parlor, I drove past our old house in Teaneck and stopped across the street. The two red maples Dad had planted when I was eight years old had grown so tall they towered over the house and cast it in cool shade. I remembered what he had said when he planted them: "Like these trees, grow as you go."

I have mementos of my father—his fishing rods, all six of them. They are precious to me.

After my father's death, I visited my mother in Florida frequently, knowing she was lonely without him. Strange, how one parent's death can bring you closer to the other one. I felt she needed a daughter to talk to, to reminisce with. Meanwhile, she threw herself into her women's sportswear and beachwear business.

My brother, Michael, still working with her, was promoted to manager, though my mother still pulled all the strings. A year after Dad died, I flew down to Florida when Mike, then thirty-two, got married. Within two years, Mom had the grandson she longed for, and two years later, a granddaughter. My mother remarried, to a retired accountant and religious cantor. It made me glad to know she had companionship once again.

* * *

One day, while I was waiting for a student to arrive for a riding lesson, Gary walked over to me and put his arm around my shoulder.

"Penny for your thoughts," he said.

"They'll cost you a quarter," I replied, grinning like the horse trader I was. Dial had stopped in his pasture and was eyeing us. Gary bent and plucked a stem of grass and sucked it for a while.

"Let's get married, Carole," he said softly.

"And live happily ever after?" I asked, smirking.

"Is that a yes?" he wanted to know, taking both my hands in his.

Smiling, I replied, "Only if you don't expect me to bake bread like your mother!"

We sealed the pact with a hug and a kiss under that denim blue sky, tears streaming down my face. Looking at Dial and then at Gary, I felt true contentment. The last pieces of my fractured jigsaw life were finally falling into place.

A big wedding was planned for the ranch hall, with guests invited from Texas to Chicago. (Alas, my mother and brother were not among the guests. They refused to attend because I was marrying a gentile. It was a sad echo of an event from my childhood: my maternal grandfather boycotting my bas mitzvah over our choice of synagogue.)

Gary's sister Sandi made the flower and table decorations. A huge flowered horseshoe the color of the blue sea was hung in front of the hall. Herb Appelin and the White Mountain Bluegrass Band played throughout the afternoon and evening, while guests danced and clapped under colored lights. Clouds of smoke drifted from the barbecue where roasts of beef, turkey, and pork turned on spits. We filled our plates with blackened meat, salads, and beans on this perfect day in June.

But not before the preacher married Gary and Carole Fletcher. Attired in a white and aqua western outfit, I sat atop Dial, who glittered in his fancy silver parade duds with a red carnation in his bridle. I could feel him beneath me, giving and trusting and kind, as if his rider got married every day. Perhaps he knew that on my third try, I had finally gotten it right.

Gary declined my offer of a mount for the ceremony, opting to stand on solid earth. He looked dapper in his Stetson hat and western garb, and he held my hand tightly as musicians on mandolin, guitar, and fiddle played while I sang to Gary the Everly Brothers tune, "Devoted to You." A tear trickled down his face.

After we exchanged vows, Gary slipped a ring on my finger, the same ring my father had slipped on my mother's finger at their wedding. Dial, of course, took a well-deserved bow. Then Gary led me away; we left the laughter and the music behind, and he showed his wedding gift to me—an exquisite four-poster cherrywood bed he had made himself and stained a rich and deep chestnut. For perhaps the first time in my whole life, I felt truly beautiful. Inside and out.

14

In Dial's Footsteps:
Heza Night Train

Singin' Saddles Ranch grew, and we grew with it. We worked, to use plain language, our butts off. Through the 1980s and well into the 1990s, Gary and I had some thirty-five horses at our place in Westmoreland. Some days the drudgery of owning all those horses had us calling it Slingin' Saddles Ranch.

As grand as the place was, the threat of becoming horse-poor spurred us on. Neither of us had a real job (although Gary period-ically took on remodeling and building jobs), so we created income in all kinds of ways. We raised Australian shepherd dogs, offered hay and sleigh rides through the seasons, put on horsemanship camps for children, offered riding lessons, horse boarding and training, and bought and sold horses. We rented out the huge ranch hall to various organizations. And in addition to Dial the Trickster, there was Carole and her dog-and-pony show.

The circus had always been a dream of mine—not the animals confined to cages and often abused (the sad side of the circus) but the magic of the big top, the clever display of animal intelligence. I brought the circus on the small scale to schools and nursing homes, birthday parties and county fairs. The act, billed as "Shorty and his Pooch Pals," featured a Shetland miniature with silver mane and tail, and dogs named Eenie, Meenie, Meinie, and Moe.

After training horses, training dogs was easy. The mixed-breed dogs (on special saddles) would take turns riding Shorty, jumping through hoops, and pushing baby carriages—standard circus fare. Shorty was fine with the dogs. It was with other horses that he showed his true colors. He was a pony, after all, and a stallion to boot. At one point I had Shorty paired with Night Train (Dial's successor, about whom I'll have more to say later), and part of the routine involved Shorty going under Night Train's legs, something they had done hundreds of times before. And while Shorty was not quite three feet tall, he acted like he was seven feet tall. One time in a show ring he dashed beneath Night Train—who is also a stallion—and bit him in the jewels.

Everyone roared. They thought it was part of the act. I could have crowned the little tempest, especially when he scooted around the ring and would not be caught. Finally, he came to me, and I made him say his prayers and beg forgiveness, as if his naughtiness were indeed part of the act. Shorty was a challenge: hard to lunge, always trying to get away with things, mischievous and stubborn. A true Shetland.

I had my own small circus for seven years, and only stopped

when we moved to Florida. Throughout the 1980s and '90s, Gary and I had been making trips to Ocala during the cold New England winters to purchase horses. Along the way, we would visit with my family. As I saw my mother aging, I yearned to spend more time with her and to lessen the miles between us. The lure of the warm Florida winters and the growing city of Ocala—"horse capital of the world"—persuaded Gary and me to move there. We were weary of plowing snow and of the bitter cold we had to work in, but one event sealed our decision to move.

The January of 1994 was like no other I had ever known—snowdrifts as high as nine feet, roofs with accumulations of three and four feet on them, bitter cold temperatures for weeks on end. To add insult to injury, heavy rains poured on the snow-covered roofs, adding dangerous weight, and finally our long-span arena buckled. The horses in the surrounding stalls were terrified, but safe. And though Gary rebuilt the arena roof—everyone in our small town pitched in for the cleanup—the collapse had soured me on snow. The Sunshine State was beckoning. Our horses, I imagined, would graze year-round.

I still have the circus-ring curb at our Florida place, all the equipment for the dogs, Shorty's old gear. You never know when the need might arise again. . . .

※　　　※　　　※

Dial would live to the ripe old age of thirty-two, an astonishing age for a horse. His death—in 1997, just before Gary and I moved to Florida—was a hard, hard blow, like losing your best friend. We buried him on that land in New Hampshire under an apple tree.

Old-timers say that you are allotted one very special horse in your lifetime. I had mine, and I sometimes think of the new owners of that farm. They are likely unaware of what lies beneath that tree. I wonder if they ever listen, just for a few seconds, if they might hear a certain horse's neigh and see through the morning mist that silliest of sights—a blue-eyed chestnut pinto smiling.

When I look at the painting of Dial hanging in my living room, I can still smell him. I look into his eyes and feel his love for me. And I can still feel him underneath me, giving me all he had.

After Dial died, I felt this powerful urge to write something about him, to pay tribute for what he had done in helping me to heal myself. I contacted *Horse & Rider* magazine, and they did a story on Dial, and that story and others led, in their way, to this book.

❊ ❊ ❊

Because Dial was about twelve when I got him, I knew that his days in the limelight were limited. I could not have imagined that he would still happily be hamming it up fifteen years later. In 1982, I was already scouting a new horse to train—an apprentice to bring along as the star aged (and to do double duty as a stallion for breeding). After looking far and wide, I found my apprentice—a blue-eyed sorrel overo paint in Cedar Hill, Missouri.

His name was Heza Night Train, and I had long admired his grandsire, a horse called Yellow Mount. The model for the first Breyer paint (Breyer makes miniature replica horses for collectors) and a supreme champion himself (the highest award in the world of paint horses), Yellow Mount was also the only paint to have sired five supreme champions: he was a legend of the breed and an astonishingly versatile horse. He could work cows, he excelled in halter and pleasure classes—he did everything.

I had spotted an ad in *Paint Horse Journal* for several of his grandsons. The owner was Roy Quinn, who worked for a brewery in St. Louis and was raising a few horses on the side. His was a small operation, yet he had raised some national champions. I liked his mild and easygoing demeanor, and he talked about his horses as if they were his children. His "star" stallion, Night Train, was a national champion and two-time congress winner.

The first time I saw Heza Night Train was in one of Roy's fields. Even from a distance, I was taken with him. Only a year old, he came running up to us, playful and whinnying and full of joy. I liked his conformation, his straight legs, his sloping shoulder and pasterns. He was—as horse people say—a nice mover. I liked his face, those alluring light blue eyes. As with Dial, there was chemistry between us. With me and horses, it's either love at first sight, or forget it. And I loved this horse. He was flashy, friendly, quiet, and calm, well mannered and well taken care of.

And, to clinch it, Heza Night Train had one white foot. An old proverb among horse people goes, "One white foot, buy 'em. Two white feet, try 'em. Three white feet, be on the sly. Four white feet, pass 'em by."

I had seen some horses in Texas earlier, but by the time I crossed the state line into New Hampshire, my mind was made up. Heza Night Train (though I soon dropped the "Heza") was coming to Singin' Saddles Ranch.

I had Jay Mele work with him. Night Train was a young stallion, after all, and I didn't yet trust my strength. Jay loved him, said he was a natural western pleasure horse—though he did have his quirks. He didn't like his ears messed with, and clipping him was a chore. And one time, Night Train got into some apples from a tree hanging over one of Jay's paddocks and began to colic. Poor Jay was beside himself, knowing what that horse meant to me. But the young stallion weathered the storm, and we avoided surgery.

Many years later—twenty, to be precise—at an equine expo in Massachusetts, I posted pictures of Night Train in my booth. Someone approached me and introduced herself as a former veterinary technician at Tufts Veterinary School.

"I know that horse!" she said, pointing at the color photograph. "I remember him. I was at Jay Mele's the night that horse colicked."

"How would you ever remember him?" I asked her.

"He was a comic," she replied. "He would smell things and curl his lips back. He'd play with his water bucket all the time, like he was a boxer using a punching bag. And his eyes, those blue eyes and those gorgeous markings. But he was easy to handle."

I told her that Night Train, after a successful show career and a national championship, had become a trick horse. "It figures," she said.

Another time, I was stabling him at a farm that hosted a show, a farm close to a railway track. That night my stallion heard the train roar past, and he went a little ballistic; so out of character for him. We all laughed. He was, after all, named Night Train.

As I write this, Night Train has been with me for twenty-one years. He mastered all the tricks that Dial did, and even went further. In the mid-1990s, the Painted Horse Saloon, a bar in Ocala—and one Gary and I used to frequent during horse-buying trips for its two-step and line dancing—was looking for a horse to act in a television commercial promoting the bar. The notion of bringing a horse into a bar may sound strange, and few horses would tolerate it. But Night Train had already seen so much—parades, camels, elephants, Ferris wheels, roller coasters.

Bellying up to the bar, amid strobe lights and loud music, and putting back—or at least appearing to—a bottle of "carrot colada," pretending to stagger and fall into a stupor with his legs crossed, Cat Ballou style: all this was no problem for him. And just at the moment when the star of the commercial was about to lift his tail and deposit something in the side pocket of the pool table, crisis was averted when Gary managed to move him along. The bar's brand-new carpet was less fortunate.

Night Train was used to lights, camera, action. A national TV commercial advertising the Citrus Bowl parade in Orlando saw me with Night Train literally wearing the stars and stripes and waving the flag. The most dramatic commercial he ever did was filmed in Atlanta for Turner Network Television's championship wrestling. It was shot in the dark, on the edge of a cliff, with simulated lightning and smoke effects and Night Train rearing at liberty. No enclosure, no lead shank. The cameras came right in on his blue eyes, but bless him, he only had eyes for me.

*   *   *

In all the years I've had him, Night Train has been a trick horse, a show horse, and a breeding stallion. He was a fussy stud, and his favorite mare was one called Angel Eyes. She was one of my favorites, too: she's a stately twenty-seven now, and she has earned her cushy retirement in a paddock next to his.

I got her from Lynn and Andrea Simons, paint horse breeders in Aubrey, Texas. Angel Eyes was six years old when I got her, and she had already been raced—in quarter-mile sprints—in California. She had some speed on her. I was looking for a versatile mare: a broodmare, a show horse, and a barrel racer.

When I first saw her, I was completely taken with her conformation, her breeding, everything. I remember when they brought her out of the barn and into the arena so I could get a closer look at her. Here was this *muscled* mare (later, at competitions, judges would double-check with me to make sure she was a mare). A shiny chestnut overo cropout—both her sire and dam were quarter horses—with beautiful blue eyes, bald face, four flashy stockings, fifteen hands high, she was picture-perfect. She was very friendly, spirited but sensible.

They saddled her, and I rode her. She was energetic, yet controlled. I watched her in the field, being lunged, being handled. This time, there was no hesitation. I had her vetted there, and I took her home in my trailer.

At home, she proved too quick and energetic for trick-horse training—though I did teach her to bow, kneel, and smile. But she proved every bit as versatile as I had hoped: she loved working with cows in competition and barrel-racing, and excelled in both, and as she got older, she became a wonderful lesson horse—especially with disabled riders. In New Hampshire, I was president of the local chapter of a riding for the disabled club, and Angel Eyes was so patient, so sensitive to those riders. She worked hard for me and earned a special place in my heart.

A friend once asked me to name the top six horses that have earned a special place in my heart. Horses I have known and loved: Bailey, Dial, Night Train, Angel Eyes, Shorty, Playboy. Every one of them has played a role in healing me. But every horse I have ever worked with has also touched my heart in one way or another. They all teach me valuable lessons every day. The love and awe I had for horses as a child remains with me to this day.

I often get letters from eleven-year-old girls who spend all their free time brushing and loving their horses—their buddies. That's real love. Then there are the people who love their horses when they win a race or ribbons. The rider never bothers to learn that this particular horse doesn't like water sprayed hard on his face, but he does like the taste of Pepsi, that he enjoys butting his feed bucket around with his head, that he dunks his hay in his water pail before eating it, that scratching him on his withers makes him stick his lips out. Such riders think their horses have no personality, but that's because they never take the time to find out. They don't see their horses as partners, but as possessions or commodities. I hope a part of me always stay eleven—for my horses' sakes.

15

In Night Train's Wake

DIAL WAS STILL YOUNG and very much the Trickster when I found myself saying, "There'll never be another Dial." And then along came Night Train, who was, and is, amazing in his own right. His successor, in turn, is the gifted young Playboy.

A seven-year-old, 15.2-hand, black-and-white overo paint stallion, Playboy is registered under the name B Mr. Playboy McQ. I bought him from Bill and Carol Mincey in Alex, Oklahoma, toward the end of 2000, when the horse was four years old. He'd been used as a breeding stallion and had about thirty days of riding on him.

I knew I wanted a black-and-white overo paint as my next trick horse, and I searched for almost two years before finding just the right one. I was particular about my requirements: he had to be athletic, responsive, kind, and curious, more than fifteen hands, with no white around the eyes and just a little white on the legs (Florida sun and sandy soil wreak havoc on white feet and can lead to melanomas).

After I'd viewed the many videos sent me, Playboy came closest to what I was looking for. I flew out to Oklahoma City and spent several days with him, observing and riding him. I instantly fell in love with this character. In his paddock he was playful with all sorts of things—buckets, lead ropes, whatever he could mouth. He was a "people" horse who loved to be rubbed; the more attention he got, the better he liked it.

Running around free, he had great moves—issuing high kicks and rears, pawing at the air, throwing his front feet out with great joie de vivre. I kept thinking that if that movement could be refined, he had all the makings of a great trick horse. Riding him clinched it for me. Though he was only "green broke" (with little formal training), he cheerfully obliged my requests.

But when I got him home, I discovered there were holes in his training. He was badly in need of ground manners. When led, he charged ahead or lagged behind me. He walked into me and failed to keep his distance. He pawed the ground impatiently. He lacked respect. He thought he was in charge, and charge he did. Playboy had been handled, bathed, and trailered a little—but not with any authority. He still wasn't sure who was boss, and in the meantime, he thought he was.

Twice daily he had his training sessions, and slowly he discovered that he was to mind me. I went about the groundwork as if I were starting from scratch with a very young colt. Without that foundation, the rest of his training would be weak. I wore out a pair of boots in those early months—walking him, backing him, and getting through the rest of the in-hand work.

Playboy always had a mischievous streak. Like Dial. He was

more "oral" than Dial, though, and liked to put cross-ties, lead ropes, and stall guards in his mouth. He'd ruin a set of reins in the blink of an eye if you turned your back on him. But he knew that human parts and clothing were off limits.

Playboy's propensity for putting things in his mouth was a boon, however, when it came time for him to fetch and retrieve objects or wave a flag. Now he has an array of toys and props that are his and his alone. His sense of mischief comes into play when I ask him to give the object back to me. For just a second, he gets that gleam in his eye, just before releasing it, as if to say, "This is mine, but well, okay, I guess you can have it. But a tug-of-war would really be fun!" His mischief keeps me on my toes, and he reminds me of myself as a child trying to get attention.

※   ※   ※

Early in the spring of 2003, and inspired by a photo of Trigger and Roy Rogers that hangs on a wall in our home, I began to work with Playboy on a challenging pose. The photo, a rare black-and-white, shows the famous horse rolled over on his back with all four feet in the air, while the celebrated cowboy's right foot rests casually on Trigger's left front hoof. I began to work daily with Playboy early in the year, enlisting the aid of a friend, Danny Jenkins. A lanky Vietnam veteran and a born raconteur with a breezy manner around horses, Danny runs a small breeding farm (Just Right Thoroughbreds) close by, certifies horses for the starting gate, and rehabilitates horses traumatized by gates.

The first task was to get Playboy to lie down, roll on his side on command, and stay there. This is an extremely vulnerable position for a horse—a flight animal by nature. That first step I accomplished myself. Rolling him onto his back was the next step, and Danny and I spent many weeks on that.

Finally, in April of that year, Playboy learned to balance and hold the pose and would allow either Danny or me to get on him and move his legs as we would a bicycle. This horse was so trusting of us that he let us do anything—even in that vulnerable pose and before an audience. I was very proud of him when we finally did it in public. When someone asked me how long it took to train Playboy for this trick, I told him two years. And it's true: it took me two years to get my horse confident, obedient, and trusting enough even to attempt this. Playboy trusts me with his life, and he performs because he wants to please me.

But there were times while training Playboy for this feat that he wasn't sure of what I wanted him to do. I was reminded of the advice offered by Ray Hunt, a respected and well-known horseman and clinician: Ask your horse to do something, make yourself clear, then get out of the way so he can do it. If I wasn't making myself clear one day with Playboy, I'd try the next. I would give my horse time to think about things.

※　　※　　※

That same spring, I performed with Night Train and Playboy before an outdoor audience of several hundred first-graders as part of a literacy project in Ocala. The kids had been reading Walter Farley's *Black Stallion* books and had come to see horses in the flesh.

Some horses love to perform, for they love applause and know that it means praise. Night Train is still like that. At the grand old age of twenty-one, my paint stallion still loves being the center of attention, and he certainly was that day at the Ocala Equestrian Complex. The first-graders had been reading in school some of Farley's other books in the series—*Little Black Goes to the Circus* and *Little Black, a Pony.* Tim Farley, Walter's son, is one backer of the literacy project, which now funds pilot programs in ten states. The idea is to instill the love of reading and combine it with an experience involving real horses.

I had my own "Little Black" on show—Playboy. But as far as these children were concerned, he was Little Black, the apprentice, with his own small array of tricks. The star of this show—and he knew it—was Night Train. Unfazed by the occasional loud crack from the microphone or the darting kids on the bleachers, he smiled for the crowd and showed off his brown teeth and nodded his head when I asked him if he had brushed this morning. He waved to the kids with one foreleg, the other on a pedestal. He spun with one front leg on the pedestal while holding the other up, as if saluting, then mounted, with all fours, the small platform. He drank, or so it seemed, from a bottle, waved the flag, bowed deeply at the end. Night Train even donned glasses and appeared to read from a book. Afterward, Night Train and Playboy stood patiently by the bleachers as the children lined up to pet them.

＊　　＊　　＊

That same year, my lower back gave out on me several times. I have, I fear, inherited my father's weak back. But during my convalescence, I thought often of Glen Randall. This wise horseman told me he had taught Trigger some seventy-eight words. This got me thinking, and, even in my frail state, acting on my thoughts.

I cannot stay away from horses in any case. Those likewise bitten by the horse bug will understand that I had to have my time with my horse—bad back and all.

I decided to exercise Playboy's fine mind. At first, my goal was to teach him to distinguish between colors. Much as I did in my teaching days, I introduced the colors red, green, blue, and yellow to him, one at a time, as I would to a child. I would ask him to touch the red bucket, the yellow bucket . . . He learned this so easily that I was encouraged to challenge him further.

With magic markers, I wrote big letters and mounted them on wooden panels. One letter at a time, I asked him to touch the *N*, then the *A*, and the *G*. (You see how my mind works.) I could not believe how quickly he learned the names of the letters! So I started to add a different task: select the mounted letter I had named aloud and bring it to me. (He already knew how to fetch and retrieve, just not with letters.)

Before long, Playboy could fetch and retrieve fifteen letters. During the 2004 Black Stallion Literacy Project in Ocala before three thousand elementary school children, he donned a pair of reading glasses and his "thinking cap" and paraded his talent by spelling *read, book,* and *cool.* Now we were sharing his talent and inspiring children, who may have been touched for a lifetime by witnessing a horse spell.

I didn't stop there. I decided to offer Playboy another challenge. With oversize playing cards, Playboy was soon picking out "a straight"—ten, jack, queen, king, ace. Now I was acting out the old cowboy's dream: I was playing cards with my horse.

I am convinced that if one horse can discriminate between colors and letters, all horses can. Albert Einstein once said that imagination is more important than knowledge. I don't think we fully appreciate or understand the minds of our domesticated animals. Who knows? This little bit of discrimination training on my part may have far-reaching implications in the horse-training world. I am reminded that you never make a discovery unless you're willing to make mistakes. Once again, my horses go on teaching me.

Meanwhile, for my own amusement, I taught my blue front Amazon parrot, Engelbird, to roller-skate. He already knows how to ride horseback. Outfitted in his bandanna and cowboy hat (air fresheners make fine bird hats), he will sit on a small saddle on a pull-toy horse, hold the reins, and say, "Giddyup!"

Since this ten-month-old parrot showed such athletic promise, I bought him a pair of birdie roller skates. Just like horse training, I proceeded by baby steps: first getting Engelbird used to standing on the skates, then moving one skate forward at a time, then the next. Reward, reward, reward. Repeat, repeat, repeat. No hurry, no time clock. Engelbird literally works for peanuts, and he has the worst case of peanut breath ever. The next project will be dunking a basketball in a hoop. Move over, Michael Jordan.

The horse world could use some of that lightening up. What bothers me more than anything about that world is not the horses but the people—and especially people who call themselves trainers.

Too often, their expectations of a horse are impossible for that horse to meet, at least in the short term. Whatever that trainer wants, he or she wants quick and easy. For me, part of the original attraction of trick-horse training was the fact that it *wasn't* quick and easy. The training was, and is, challenging, demanding, consuming. It's like anything worthwhile—playing music, learning to read. It's a slow, step-by-step process.

I also came to see trick-horse training as an alternative to the high seriousness and cutthroat competition of the show ring—something I had seen firsthand. The trick horse may never perform for anyone other than his rider and a few stablemates. Or he may perform before millions on television or before thousands in a live audience—all of whom are judging him.

Whether the stage is small or large, what is undeniable is this: first, the horse taught tricks is a brighter, more interesting horse; and second, the horse becomes a more responsive horse by paying attention to the trainer's cues.

A bored horse, an underutilized horse, is not a happy horse. Tricks enrich a horse's life by stimulating his mind and by sending both work and praise his way. You'll see the results in the stable, on the trail, and in the show ring. The horse will endear himself to those who see him, and his value will increase. The bond between horse and rider strengthens. Twenty-five years of trick-horse training have taught me those truths.

❋　　❋　　❋

There may never be another horse like Playboy in my life. But I choose to believe that there will be—that my skill, and a little luck in choosing, will mean my barn will have a trick horse as long as I'm fit enough to keep him busy.

Lately, I've been working with Peruvian Paso horses, gaited horses with great sensitivity. I'm enamored of their responsiveness, and I find myself daydreaming about starting another young horse. I always like to think there's another horse on the horizon.

One Peruvian Paso horse I'm working with near our home in Florida is a four-year-old liver chestnut stallion with a two-foot-long flaxen mane, and a tail to match. His proper name is Patriarca, though I call him Patchie. A stable hand at the big farm where I work the horse six days a week confided to me that this one had been a real outlaw before I started working with him (nobody had mentioned that to me *before* I started working with him). This young horse was no outlaw, just extremely sensitive and concerned about everything. The stable hand wondered what my magic was. No magic. Just a lot of time, love, and a willingness to listen to what makes that horse happy and confident.

Part of my method involves getting up at 5:30 so I can be at his barn by 7:00 A.M. Patchie hasn't been fed by that time, and he *really* wants those carrots. I don't know who is more enthusiastic—him or me. If he gets overeager and butts my hand for a treat, I need only look at him and scold him, "Now, Patchie, unh, unh, unh." He knows he's been bad, and he backs away, wanting to make peace. The carrot accord asserts itself, and we get back to work. Still, he is often impatient, and when he is, I have to slow him down by standing around a lot and making him wait.

Patriarca is also a horse who needs to be groomed just so, or he becomes agitated. His mouth is shallow and tender, so he needs a bit he finds comfortable—the less severe, the better. He needs to be pushed, but if pushed too much, he becomes resentful. He has to be disciplined, but not harshly. The iron fist in velvet glove works best with him. Patriarca needs to be given consistent limits and guidance. He needs, above all, what all horses need and what all humans crave: to be treated like an individual and to have his idiosyncracies respected and acknowledged. This all sounds very much like child-rearing.

Like the master horseman John Lyons, who revolutionized horse training, I handle the horse respectfully, encouraging him to yield to slight pressure. I teach him to move his feet forward, backward, and to each side; to bend his neck and flex at the poll; to turn on his haunches and forehand. These maneuvers relax the horse's body and soften his mind. They also teach the horse to have control over his body. It's all groundwork, preparation for under-saddle work.

On several occasions in the New Hampshire days, I met Glen Randall, and he would always say that if you get angry or impatient working with a horse, walk away. You'll take a step backward if you don't. Have a coffee, he'd say. Sit and think on it. In more than twenty years of trick-horse training, I can honestly say that I've never felt defeated by a horse. I've always followed Glen's advice: I sleep on it, go back to it later. Above all, I give the horse time.

❋   ❋   ❋

Time, it seems, is in short supply. Horses at the racetrack know that better than any. When we race two-year-old Thoroughbreds, for example, we are literally racing babies. And I am not alone in thinking this.

Dr. Deb Bennett is part of the Equine Studies Institute in Livingston, California—a colloquium of experts who share the same approach to horsemanship. They host clinics and write on horse anatomy, conformation, biomechanics, and riding technique. Dr. Bennett, for one, has argued that no horse is mature before the age of six (plus or minus six months).

She notes the old saying that before riding a young horse for the first time, it's best to wait "until his knees close." The saying reflects an equine physiological truth: it's best to wait until the horse's growth plates fuse to the bone shaft and cease to be separated from it by mere cartilage.

Physiologically, then, it makes no sense to race very young horses. The only possible sense it makes is economic—these two-year-old horses, though immature, are nonetheless fast. And while the odds against winning are high (90 percent of racehorse owners lose money), the fat purses must seem irresistible. Owners can't wait to get their two-year-olds into the starting gate in hopes of recouping the huge sums already spent on purchase fees, board, trainers' and grooms' wages, vet and farrier bills.

It's sad to say, but money makes the world go 'round, greed makes babies run, and speed sells. I wish it were not so.

For more than two decades, I have taught horses, and horses have taught me.

In New England, for example, I worked with Scott Bassi, a thirteen-year-old boy with Down syndrome. I paired Scott with a paint mare named Cheyenne Spring, a push-button older horse.

Scott took lessons on her for a year, and that fall, at the Labor Day Fair in Guilford, Vermont, he got a first-place ribbon, beating out twenty other unchallenged riders. It brings tears to my eyes just to think about it. He had no concept of what he had done. I was so overcome with joy, as were his parents.

Two days later, I had to take Cheyenne Spring to a veterinary hospital in Cornell; the mare had cancer, but there was nothing they could do. That fair was her last hurrah, the blue ribbon her parting gift to Scott. The trailer came back to the farm empty. Scott could not understand where Cheyenne Spring had gone; he went up and down the row of stalls, looking for her. He had no concept of death, no more than he had a concept of victory. He later took more lessons on another paint, and his parents bought him a horse that resembled Cheyenne Spring. Later he got a job in a stable, and his mother was convinced that what he had learned from horses helped him live independently. Cheyenne had taught him many valuable lessons.

That story totally resonates with mine. Horses taught me about hope and independence and so much else—because each horse has a distinct personality and capacity for learning. A horse teaches you to be clear. Another lesson is persistence: how to be calm and consistent. Horses became my teachers, and this book is a way of thanking them and keeping alive their memory.

I will have horses in my life as long as I am able. In *Talking of Horses,* Monica Dickens writes, "When I can't ride anymore, I shall keep horses as long as I can hobble about with a bucket and a wheelbarrow. When I can't hobble, I shall roll my wheelchair out to the fence of the field where my horses graze and watch them."

Whether by wheelbarrow or wheelchair, I will do likewise to keep alive—as long as I can and as best I can—my connection with horses.

*   *   *

Late in April of 2004, I did what I had long been thinking about: I bought a Peruvian Paso horse.

His name is Magnifico, and he is truly that. Magnificent. He looks very much like Patriarca, only taller and with a much longer mane. This five-year-old stallion is 15.1 hands, a liver chestnut with a three-foot-long flaxen mane, and a tail that sweeps the ground. And sweet, sweet, sweet. Stallions can be difficult and unruly, but you'd never know Magnifico was a stud.

He came to me as if it were destined. I had heard about a dispersal sale near our farm. A woman was selling her herd of thirty-five Peruvian horses, all the tack and equipment—everything—after her husband died of a brain tumor. The prices were cheap, and the auctioneer informed all of us would-be buyers that it was "an absolute auction." Everything must sell.

I had gone to the farm the day before and looked at two horses, but I was especially drawn to Magnifico. When he went up on the block, my heart pounded long and hard. I shrieked when it was announced that he was sold to me. All the folks from Patriarca's stable were on hand, and they were all ecstatic for me. Gary nearly had to revive me.

During the next week, Magnifico and I began getting acquainted, slowly, with lots of groundwork. He reminds me of Dial in a way. He has that kind of responsiveness. You think it, he does it. If Playboy is manual, this fellow is automatic. Playboy, poor man, is *very* jealous. He kicks his stall door for my attention.

It seems I have fallen in love with another animal. I tell friends that Gary may not see another home-cooked meal until Christmas. He knows where to find me.

Ah, life is good.

16

Looking Back

ONE DAY IN late fall of 2003, or what passes for fall here in Florida, I cut a sizable red apple in half and laid the two pieces facedown on the cutting board that graces the kitchen counter here, as it did for so long in New Hampshire. I love the board's wide oval shape, the thin alternate strips of walnut and maple, dark wood and light, that run its width and give the old cutting board a curious, two-toned vigor—as if the wood were somehow still alive.

That day I stood at the counter and paused before slicing the apple further, before slipping the pieces into the fanny pack at my waist and heading out to the horse barn. That day, November 22, 2003, would be a day full of pauses, for it marked a grim anniversary. On that same date, a Saturday in 1975, my life changed.

I was twenty-eight years old then, and twenty-eight years have since transpired. I'm fifty-six as I write these words, so the two halves of the apple struck me that day as a tidy metaphor. The half on my left represented life before the fire; its twin on the right, life after. I stared long and hard at those two half globes and pondered the two blocks of time they stood for. There is no middle in my life, only the time before the fire and the time after.

I continue to feel, almost three decades later, a sense of loss from the transforming event in my life. The lament is still there. Always.

Seven years after the fire, I was part of an NBC-TV special about disfigured women called *For Beauty Passed Away*. Did you know that the city of Chicago, in 1881, passed an "Ugly Ordinance"—"that any person, disfigured, maimed, mutilated, deformed, unsightly or disgusting shall not expose himself to public vew in public places"? The law remained on the books until 1973.

We remain fixed on some ideal of beauty. Witness a reality TV series in 2004 called *The Swan:* women submit to plastic surgeons, dentists, and personal trainers, are diced and sliced, tucked and enhanced, chiseled and polished, like cars in a body shop. The transformed "ugly ducklings" then compete in a beauty pageant. The women do it because they can't accept themselves.

There is a part of me that feels grateful for what befell me. I look back at that old *My Fair Lady* photograph and think how shallow and superficial that young woman was, how much she squirmed under the thumb of her domineering mother, how adrift she was. That day in the basement—in that moment of searing heat and blinding blue light, in the *whoooomp* of combustion—everything changed.

For years, my questions were, Why was I chosen for this? What did I do to deserve this? Am I being punished? Only later would I begin to ask other questions. What have I learned from all this? What can others take from it?

I am a better person because of the accident. This is no heresay, no blind optimism, but hard-won truth. You never know what you're made of until you're tested and made to struggle some. The struggle makes you better. I'm stronger mentally, physically, emotionally. The accident put a turn in my life, and yes, there was a great loss. Almost thirty years after the accident, the fire continues to plague me in smaller ways: the skin grafts on my feet left me without feeling there, and the paper-thin skin is prone to sores. Shoes are a problem. And though I am comfortable around fire, I cannot bear to watch a movie about fire—especially involving children. A stuntman on fire triggers terrible flashbacks. And years of medical interference would scar me. My great fear now is that I will contract some sort of chronic illness that will keep me in a hospital indefinitely. Enough is enough. Even going to the doctor is hard for me now.

But despite all that, the fire left me with a tremendous gain in wisdom. When your life is hanging by a thread, you ask, What is important? What haven't I done? Time suddenly becomes precious.

Now every day in my life is a special gift. I spend more time with my family, and express my love to family members. I no longer save things for special occasions. I use my "good" china every day. I put on my special perfume when I feel like it, not just for special occasions. I wear new clothes to a horse show. I want to listen, see, do—*now*. The word *someday* has faded from my vocabulary. Because someday may never come. It might be taken from you. Just like that.

I am fond of this tiny parable: A man is granted one question when God appears before him. "How much time do I have," the man asked, "before I die?" "Enough time," God answers, "to make a difference." This is my hope: that my story, my book, will make a difference in someone's life.

The horse did not heal me. It's *working* with horses that heals, by developing discipline, courage, patience, and perseverance. You may come to horses—as I did—unable to walk, unable to cope, disfigured and in despair, but what I learned is that horses do not judge by looks or class or reputation. Still, you must earn their trust and cooperation, and out of that comes self-esteem. I tell people about how painfully slow schooling can be, but how thrilling it is when the horse starts to understand, to perform on cue and take satisfaction from his work.

When *Horse & Rider* magazine chronicled my story in 1998, they called it "Burning Desire," the piece fronted by a shot of me on Dial rearing on cue. Both horse and rider appear to be enjoying themselves; both are wearing a smile.

*   *   *

If this book acknowledges my debt to horses, may it also honor the role played in my recovery by the people close to me. My mother, my husband.

My mother first. She will not be pleased, I know, to see her age revealed in these pages. On the other hand, she has mellowed a great deal in her later years, discovered a playfulness she never showed in her youth, and we sometimes do what once seemed unthinkable to me: we go on vacations together. You could write a book about our relationship; pity the right title—*War and Peace*—has already been taken. After many decades in battle, we have found the way to a cease-fire; Gary and I moved to Florida, in part, to allow me more time with her. It has taken fifty-six years, but mother and daughter finally get on.

At her store, my mother retains her way with numbers and details. She is still the boss, her sister Rose still works alongside her at the age of ninety-one, and my brother remains her longtime employee. After one year of college, Michael took a job as a clerk in a drugstore; then my mother took him into her business. His two young children visit me several times a year for what seems to them the best sort of riding camp. My mother, meanwhile—even as she approaches her ninth decade—appears reluctant to turn over the reins to anyone. On the other hand, she has finally accepted Gary as her son-in-law.

Today, I continue to feel a glow in the company of this small man with the gray in his hair and the gravel in his voice. Gary has what horse people call "a kind eye"—and a draft horse's appetite for work. In some ways, he is still the kid sharpening chain saws at midnight for ten cents a week. And though I feign shock, I actually like Gary's sometimes naughty jokes, and I forgive him his occasional Archie Bunker outbursts.

I'm Gary's number-one fan. He overcame an abusive, alcoholic father, and did it without bitterness. He came out of dire poverty, and found humor in that. He really is an inspiration. A ball cap, sweatshirt, and jeans sort of guy, Gary is less voluble when it comes to declaring his affection. He is more likely, and this point bears repeating, to build something as a declaration of his affection. All items could bear the same plaque: "This is dedicated to the one I love."

When, as part of the process of this memoir, I began writing down the details of my life, including details of my accident, I showed it to Gary for his thoughts. But he couldn't bear to read about my suffering. That's the kind of man he is.

Gary has embarked on a remarkable spate of building projects around our farm in Florida: a huge and formidably tall workshop ("It's an aircraft hangar," one friend teased him). A six-stall barn. And the best fifty-foot covered round pen I have ever seen.

Most of the round pens around Ocala are utilitarian jobs made of concrete or wood. Gary's is a work of art, fashioned of southern yellow pine and engineered along the same lines as an umbrella. Early in construction, a heavy beam ran from the ground to the peak of the round pen's roof—twenty-four feet in the air. When all the supporting trusses were in place, Gary neatly cut the beam off at the roof—and the many ribs of that great umbrella of course held fast. When I am in the center of the round pen, working with Playboy, friends looking on are often drawn to the roof. It is like being in a medieval cathedral in France: you always want to look up, in awe.

Visitors to the Fletcher ranch say they are struck by our abiding belief in work and our abiding faith in craft. Nothing here is done in slipshod fashion. The training of trick horses, the building of round pens: it is all done to an exceedingly high standard. We take the time to do it right.

※　　　※　　　※

As I look back on my life, one moment gives me particular satisfaction. In 1992 I got a call from my old friend, Harry Gaynor, of the National Burn Victim Foundation, inviting me to do a promotion for National Fire Prevention Week. He asked me to speak at the Hackensack Medical Center (the hospital had expanded and changed its name) in New Jersey, my virtual home for seven months.

This time I took Dial. On the tarmac outside the hospital where helicopters land with patients, we entertained an audience of two hundred staff members and patients. Looking on were incredulous doctors and nurses, many of whom had tended to me there almost seventeen years beforehand. Dr. Barbara was there, and nurse Toni Kardell. With tears in her eyes and a huge smile, she told me she'd never seen a patient recover so well and that the sight of me on my horse made her life's work seem eminently worthwhile. I credited my horses—Bailey and Dial—with my recovery. As I hoisted young burn victims onto Dial's back, I made my message loud and clear: "I did it, and you can, too. Believe in yourself."

For ten consecutive years after the fire, I would call the burn unit at Hackensack Hospital every November 22nd—to say hello, to tell them how I was making out, and to learn what staff were still there. I had been so long in that place that it had begun to feel a little like home. I was calling to touch base. Nevertheless, I had vowed never to go back to a burn unit. But on Monday, December 8, 2003, a little more than twenty-eight years after the fire, I broke that vow. I made the visit I had been dreading, a visit made necessary by the writing of this book.

I went to the burn unit at Shands Hospital, part of the University of Florida at Gainesville, about thirty miles north of Ocala. Gary was away working, and so I asked a friend to accompany me. I wasn't sure I could face going alone.

We were given a tour by the head nurse, a cheerful fortyish black woman named Joyce Welch, who has worked in the eight-bed unit for twenty years. Her sense of commitment and dedication to burn care are remarkable. Why, I asked her, have you stayed so long in this unit? Here, she said, there is a sense of familiarity: "We're like family."

Joyce explained that with only eight patients in the unit, and often for several months, she comes to know each patient's family—the patient's moral support—very well. Families are allowed to bring in home-cooked meals as a welcome change from hospital fare. Such an arrangement is better for the patient; better for the family, too, who are made to feel part of the recovery team.

The nursing staff try very hard to get the patient's family involved in boosting the patient's will to live. The wife of a young black man in the burn unit had made a tape of his children's voices, each one begging him to get better and play with them. That man would listen to the tape every day as his dressings were changed. "In this unit," said Joyce, "as in the one you were in, we never say 'I can't.' We say, 'We will.' "

I kept sniffing the air, trying to identify some of the same smells I would have known at Hackensack. But there were none that I could discern. No doubt had I lingered I would have picked up the smell of alcohol (used with needles and IVs), saline for dressing changes, and the smells of medication and ointments on wounds. If there was a smell at all to the burn unit at Shands Hospital, I would say it smelled clean—antiseptic clean, sterile clean.

The corridors in the burn unit were empty, but its walls were full: diagrams and text on first-, second-, and third-degree burns, pictures of young children having fun at burn camps, framed newspaper clippings of former patients who had recovered from their burns. The message: There is, indeed, life after burns.

"So much has changed," said Joyce, "since you were in the hospital. I'll show you."

The new approach to burns is highly aggressive. Waiting weeks for dead, burned skin to separate on its own before starting grafting—that's out. The new approach calls for early excision and grafting, using skin taken from tiny areas, skin which is then cultured and grown. Feeding has also changed dramatically: a feeding tube is inserted immediately into the patient's gut, rather than intravenously, as had been done with me. I had lost a third of my weight in a matter of weeks; today, burn patients typically lose only 10 percent of their body weight.

Contractures such as those on my left hand, ankles, and toes are now avoided by plastic splinting and immediate physical therapy. Gone, too, are the metal splints and pins used in my feet, as well as the rotating bed.

The new approach to burns is a team approach, with burn surgeons, an anesthesiologist, a psychologist, a chaplain, a dietician, a physical therapist, an occupational therapist, a social worker, and of course nurses, all part of a team that often gathers in the conference room, and even has lunch together when there's time. Two or three nurses are assigned to each patient to change dressings every shift, but each patient also has one special nurse assigned to him or her every shift.

But some things are the same. The stained sheets, for example. Scarlet red is used on donor sites—those places on the patient's body where skin is harvested. The red stains the sheets, and all laundry coming from, and going to, the burn unit invariably features those red stains. No bleach will remove it. White sheets with red stains: it's the mark of a burn unit. The slow morphine drips have not changed either. The sight of them took me back to Hackensack. I tell people now I had two favorite drugs in those days: Demerol and Damnitall.

And while a burn unit will always be about pain, I was overjoyed to learn that the greatest contributor to my pain was now obsolete. The dreaded Hubbard tank, which I had dubbed "Old Mother Hubbard," was no more. I was thrilled that showers had replaced it.

In his office, the burn unit's surgeon, Dr. David Barillo, explained why. The Hubbard tank, it was eventually learned, contained "bacterial soup." Infection was being passed on from patient to patient, and so the immersion process was replaced by shower carts suspended over the tank. The new way meant less heat loss and less stress for patients, and required far fewer medical staff.

Dr. Barillo spoke with a familiar accent. A former volunteer with fire departments in New Jersey, he knew both Dr. Barbara and Harry Gaynor and had been to the burn unit at Hackensack (five beds then, twenty-four now). At one point he took from a shelf in his office a medical text—*Burns: A Team Approach*—published in 1979. Inside was a black-and-white photograph of a patient on a metal cot being submersed in that hated tank. It was shiny stainless steel, a ten-foot-wide oval, and tank and patient were ringed by nurses. That patient, I thought, could have been me. My gut churned at the thought.

For weeks after I left the burn unit, I hardly slept. I felt like a war veteran suffering flashbacks. What kept running through my mind were images from the burn unit and the photographs from that medical text. My mind was reeling from all I had seen.

It staggers the mind that twenty-eight years after my accident, some two thousand fires a year in America involve gas-powered water heaters. More than three hundred people a year are burned in such fires, many of them terribly. Is it possible that hot-water-heater manufacturers and gas companies believe it's cheaper to settle these cases out of court than to go to the trouble and expense of ensuring that each water heater is equipped with a properly functioning safety device? A simple antivapor mechanism would automatically shut off the pilot light in the presence of flammable fumes. So much pain and heartache would be spared.

In the meantime, some 60 million American homes have gas-fired water heaters, and the number of people burned in preventable accidents continues to mount. Whatever the cause of burns, the outcome is often horrific. Of those burned, between eight thousand and twelve thousand will die, making burns a leading cause of death in America—surpassed only by automobile accidents and falls. Burn victims are very much an invisible population. External scars, they hide with long sleeves and long pants; psychological scars are not so easily masked. Some burn survivors simply retreat behind closed blinds, for the stares and the pity are too much to bear.

Hanging on the patio doors at our place in Florida is a stained-glass window: a striking peacocklike bird with gorgeous blue-green plumage arising out of orange and yellow flames and looking toward a cloud-dotted sky. The work of Rick Neumann, a Vermont craftsman, the piece is precious to me. It was one of the few things I took from our house in New Hampshire. Every time I walk outside to the patio, to water my many potted plants at dawn, to swim at dusk, I see that phoenix. In a way, I *am* that phoenix.

* * *

I hope that there will always be a horse in my barn, and in my life. That the magic feeling for horses I felt as a child will stay with me until my time is up. That I will always be "home on the reins."

I have even imagined my perfect death. I am galloping a horse, and we both leave this life in the same blink of an eye, my horse of a heart attack, me by breaking my neck—the sort of demise that Winston Churchill, who loved horses and riding, once described as "a very good death to die." I even have a date in mind: November 22, 2035, by which time I will be eighty-eight years old.

And maybe a kindly obit writer will grace my mention with a pun (or two), then offer the view that the old girl not only rose from the ashes but had a pretty good ride after the fire.

Epilogue

by LAWRENCE SCANLAN

WE LIVE IN A CULTURE that prizes youth and beauty, and Carole Fletcher apparently lost both in a heartbeat on the morning of November 22, 1975. In the wake of the fire, she walked like an old and feeble woman, and she no longer felt beautiful, but ugly. Uncommonly, unspeakably, unbearably ugly.

In her book, *Autobiography of a Face,* Lucy Grealy describes what it was like—at the age of nine—to have a third of her jaw removed. The pain of feeling ugly, she observed, "I always viewed as the great tragedy of my life. The fact that I had cancer seemed minor in comparison."

But like Carole Fletcher, Lucy Grealy found consolation in horses. "My one real source of relief," she called them. At the age of fourteen, Grealy got a summer job as a stable hand, and she would discover that while horses never resolved her pain, they did give her time, time to muster the courage she would need to face the staring world. "Horses," she wrote, "neither disapproved nor approved of what I looked like. All that counted was how I treated them."

Alone in the barn, Grealy would rest her head on a horse's flank, trace the whorls in his hide with the fingers of one hand, and rest the other hand on the soft skin of his belly. "All the while, I'd listen to the patient sounds of their stomachs and smell the sweet air from their lungs as attentively as if I were being sent information from another world."

The British writer Monica Dickens likewise observes, "A horse has the headiest, most satisfying scent of all animals. . . . A horse's breath is a mixture of warm apples and chicken soup."

Jane Smiley, the Pulitzer Prize–winning author, had been a horse-mad teenager. Then, in midlife, she was snared again when her nose did her in: "The moment was Proustian—I walked into a stable, and smelled the sweet, sour, green, moist richness of muck and it filled me with longing." Smiley would later write a novel called *Horse Heaven*.

Carole Fletcher, Lucy Grealy, Monica Dickens, Jane Smiley: all women. There is something between women and horses, girls and horses, that warrants examination. In her book *Dark Horses and Black Beauties: Animals, Women, a Passion,* Melissa Holbrook Pierson lists some numbers on females and horses (this was a few years ago). The U.S. Pony Club, she noted, has fourteen thousand members; four-fifths are girls. In the United States Dressage Federation, 95 percent are female.

Dark Horses and Black Beauties is a fresh, original work. Here is Pierson on what attracts us to the horse: "So it is first the way they look, both to and at us, that pins us flat. It is a magisterial beauty. . . . They are a stirringly impossible mixture of power and delicacy, size and fragility. They inspire fear even as they are filled with it themselves. They are wild and they are utterly tamable." Pierson comes finally to the eyes—among the largest in the animal kingdom— "great pools of assessment and expression" that she believes draw us in, appealing at some deep and primitive level to our desire to nurture.

*   *   *

A growing body of literature has examined how animals—horses in particular—can help people who are severely damaged in physical and psychological ways. The authors of *Horse Sense and the Human Heart,* for example, are a mother-daughter team of psychologists in California named Adele and Deborah McCormick. One case, in particular, led them to write their book.

John was a virtually mute, severely depressed schizophrenic whom the McCormicks assigned to work with a Welsh pony named Cricket. As the man's horse-handling skills grew, so did his confidence: he would eventually find work with horses and go on to earn a degree in English. "We had always felt horses were special companions," the authors wrote. "After seeing John's transformation, we started seeing them in another light—as potent agents of change."

Lucy Grealy came to the same conclusion: horses are good medicine.

Increasingly, these are the questions being asked: How can animals help us? Does the act of reaching out to our fellow creatures, or simply taking the time to observe and communicate with them, make us more fully human? Are we made healthier, happier, stronger, by such meaningful contact?

The medical benefits of having an animal companion are well documented. Heart patients, Alzheimer's patients, and troubled adolescents seem to benefit from contact with animals. People with pets report a greater sense of psychological well-being, and typically get far more exercise than those without animals. Simply watching fish in an aquarium, petting a dog, grooming a horse: all lower blood pressure.

When the help that animals offer is not incidental, but planned and prescriptive, it has a name: pet therapy (coined in 1969 by American child psychiatrist Boris Levinson) or, its modern equivalent, animal-assisted therapy. When horses are called upon to help heal humans, it's called hippotherapy. But what feels new and radical is not; the ancient Greeks practiced a modest version of hippotherapy. Soldiers wounded in war would be set on the back of a walking horse to help them recover, for the Greeks knew that the small act of sitting a horse and rolling with the motion seems to massage every ache and every limb.

Today, animals play therapeutic roles in psychiatric institutions, nursing homes, and prisons all over the world. Some thirty-six American states use animals in their prisons in some rehabilitative way—from wild horses to dogs, cats, fish, birds, mice, and pigs.

Every year, the number of programs that use horses to help humans grows by leaps and bounds. Today, there are more than six hundred therapeutic riding centers affiliated with the North American Riding for the Handicapped Association (NARHA), and countless more unlisted programs. Carole Fletcher, you will remember, found a deep satisfaction in New England by connecting challenged riders with her horses.

In all of these programs, the hope is not of the faint kind, but more and more rooted in measurable results. They seem a natural fit, the words *horse* and *healing*.

※   ✧   ✿

There is a life force about Carole Fletcher. The eyes have it. It's there in that quick-shuffle walk of hers, the animation when she talks about her life with horses, how she finds cause to sing the praises of those in her circle. On one my visits to Singin' Saddles, I learned that her friend and fellow trick-horse trainer, Gina Allison (who learned her craft by watching and helping Carole), also makes ingenious pop-up cards and sends them to friends at Christmas, and no recipient was more appreciative than Carole Fletcher.

She does not bestow flattery; the praise is heartfelt and genuine. And for someone who is so at home in the spotlight—not all who love center stage are so inclined—Carole is remarkably generous.

On the last day of my visit, en route to the airport in Orlando, I asked Gina about her sprawling family—she has seven siblings, as I do, and was raised in rural Louisiana. Well, she said, there's Belle and Tinker . . .

"Gina"—I stopped her—"those are the names of draft horses!"

"Well, yes," she drawled (they really do say in the bayous "Say what?" and "I tell you what!" and speak at the speed of running molasses). "And at one point ma mother was going to name one of us after the mule, but she thought there'd be some confusion."

I thought Carole was going to drive off the freeway, she was laughing so hard. She kept on saying how witty we both were, how creative, and the more she said it, the more we were inclined to believe her. This must be what it's like to be a horse under the tutelage of Carole Fletcher. The horse starts to feel good about himself, understood and appreciated, smart and capable—as Carole herself is—of almost anything.

Acknowledgments

THE DEATH OF DIAL, my beloved horse, led to this book. Writing it was, on the one hand, gut-wrenching, and on the other hand, a healing experience. What sustained me throughout was the conviction that my story could help others facing adversity. Call it destiny, but this book was meant to be. My pleas for help early on were answered when many angels were sent my way.

The first was Elly Sidel, my literary agent, who believed in me from the start and who guided me through the roller-coaster ride of getting the idea for the book to a publisher. You have a wonderful story, Elly would say, but the writing needs help.

Enter the second angel, Lawrence Scanlan, an artist with words and a knowledgeable horseman. Larry's thought-provoking questions challenged me to critically examine what I had written in my first draft. He nursed me through gruelling draft after draft. To Larry (and his horse Dali) I owe this book.

More angels came in the form of the enthusiastic editors (with readable handwriting!) at Atria: Tracy Behar and Wendy Walker. Their insightful comments compelled me to be even more introspective. Their critical eyes and patience with me were invaluable. Tracy and Wendy took this book by the hand and helped it find its way into the world. The book's copy editor was Miranda Ottewell, who made some nice catches.

My gratitude extends to the photographers and book designers who gave the book character and style. In particular, I want to mention Chris Sartre, Michelle Younghans, and Sherry Barker. They came to Singin' Saddles Ranch and captured my horses on film. Some of the horses are gone now, but their images live on and I treasure them.

Many family members and friends helped to shape this book, cheering me on. First and foremost is my mother, Jene Rosenberg Kugler. Were it not for her recollections on tape and personal interviews, this book would have been leaner. Next, my cherished husband and partner, Gary Fletcher, who shared with me many vivid memories of people and horses. Because of him, my precious animals are safely stabled, fenced, and watered. Gary has always encouraged my passion for horses, listened to my tales about them, and tolerated me shutting out the world while I wrote about them. I also want to thank other family members for sharing their own memories with me: Michael Rosenberg, Charles Rosenberg, Norma Cybul, Anita Dahlia, Harold Rosenberg, Justine Trueger Bruner, Susan Grabow, Sandi Fletcher Gantz, Ron Fletcher, and Rose Kushner.

Many others also helped along the way, patiently answering my endless questions: Don Goldman; Beryl Goldbaum; Harry Gaynor (now deceased); Kathy Pinera; Dr. David Barillo and Joyce Welch at Shands Hospital, University of Florida; and Diana Ohme at Hackensack Medical Center. I am also indebted to the outstanding staff who treated me after the fire in the burn unit at Hackensack Hospital.

Finally, heartfelt thanks to my horses and those of others, whose unconditional love and acceptance and willingness to please both inspire and teach me every day of my life.